Peter O. Stecher

Legends in Archery

Adventurers with Bow and Arrow

"We were no longer, technically, children although in many ways I am quite sure that we were…but to have the heart of a child is not a disgrace. It is an honor."

–Ernest Hemingway, *True at First Light*

Schiffer Publishing Ltd
4880 Lower Valley Road Atglen, Pennsylvania 19310

Other Schiffer Books on Related Subjects:

***The Bow Builder's Book: European Bow Building from the Stone Age to Today*, 978-0-7643-2789, $34.95**

***Bow Accessories*, 978-0-7643-3035-3, $34.99**

Library of Congress Control Number: 2010932462

Type set in: Minion Pro
ISBN: 978-0-7643-3575-4
Printed in China

Schiffer Books are available at special discounts for bulk purchases for sales promotions or premiums. Special editions, including personalized covers, corporate imprints, and excerpts can be created in large quantities for special needs. For more information contact the publisher:

Published by Schiffer Publishing Ltd.
4880 Lower Valley Road
Atglen, PA 19310
Phone: (610) 593-1777; Fax: (610) 593-2002
E-mail: Info@schifferbooks.com

For the largest selection of fine reference books on this and related subjects, please visit our web site at

www.schifferbooks.com

We are always looking for people to write books on new and related subjects. If you have an idea for a book please contact us at the above address.

This book may be purchased from the publisher.
Include $5.00 for shipping.
Please try your bookstore first.

You may write for a free catalog.

In Europe, Schiffer books are distributed by
Bushwood Books
6 Marksbury Ave.
Kew Gardens
Surrey TW9 4JF England
Phone: 44 (0) 20 8392 8585; Fax: 44 (0) 20 8392 9876
E-mail: info@bushwoodbooks.co.uk
Website: www.bushwoodbooks.co.uk

Contents

Foreword

Dear readers,

It is a big thing for an Austrian author when his book is published internationally. Pete Schiffer of Schiffer Publishing helped me make it possible—thanks! Karin Dorner-Schermann, a friend and extraordinarily clever woman, translated my German scribbling for the English-speaking reader. She is an accurate and skilful translator. She is not an archer, but to work on my book she needed the appropriate background knowledge and read many bow and arrow classics from my library. And now it looks like she might have a severe form of archery fever, too. Thanks, Karin.

This book emanated from my desire to let today's archers experience the adventures and the spirit of archery pioneers, and maybe to motivate them to learn more and to read the many wonderful books written by these fascinating characters. It looks like traditional bowmen are a worldwide brotherhood—many archers and experts helped me whenever I had questions. My thanks to Michael Sarnitz and Alois Zopf, legends in Austrian archery. Michale Sarnitz is still in contact with me, sharing news about archery from his travels around the world.

I did not choose the "legends" described in this book by rating them. My selection depended entirely on whether I could find accurate and complete information and acquire the books with the relevant facts.

English-speaking, and for the most part, American archers, should be credited with making archery, and bowhunting in particular, as popular as it is today. We cannot speak of a uniform archery tradition in Austria, Germany, or Europe. I believe archery in the United States is less based on Native American archery, but more a continuation of the British tradition. However, it did not remain a lawn sport for high society in "wild" America. The bow and arrow, whether used for competitions or hunting, became the tools of the trade for a certain breed of men and women—those who cherished camaraderie, the love of nature, and adventure. I corresponded with many archers, always recognizing that theses values are worth preserving

Finally, I'd like to apologize for being so presumptuous. I hope not to come across as an Austrian lecturing Americans on "their" pioneers. My goal was to work carefully and accurately to write an enjoyable book, a book where you can meet many "legends" at the "virtual campfire," like the heroes of ancient times in "Valhalla." Let's listen to the tales of their adventures…

Peter O. Stecher
Lockenhaus, Austria

Acknowledgements

My thanks to my daughters, Elisabeth and Johanna, for their patience. While working on the book, playing with bows, arrows, various other weapons, and reading many books, I was not much of a companion.

A great number of friends have made this book possible. In no particular order and without considering this list exhaustive, I am deeply indebted to the following: my Austrian publisher Dr. Dietmar Vorderegger. It was a great pleasure when he, trusting my opinion and intuition, published this book. My thanks are also due to Pete Schiffer for publishing the book internationally.

I thank Fred Anderson, John Schulz, and Craig Ekin of Howard Hill Archery; Byron Ferguson; T.J. Conrads, editor of the *Traditional Bowhunter* Magazine; and all the others who readily gave permission to use illustrations or information from their books and answered questions that were important to my research.

And my thanks are given, too, to Cliff Huntington, Bob Wesley, John D. Lee, Gene Wensel, Wade Phillips, and John D. Vasos for their patience and for giving their generous and free advice and assistance, motivated by their passion for the bow and arrow.

Ted Fry of Raptor Archery, Oregon, a swell guy, sent me pictures of Sasha Siemel's, Howard Hill's, and Hugh Rich's bows and archery tackle. Thank you, Ted!

Sondra Siemel from Pennsylvania, daughter of Sasha Siemel, provided helpful and additional information on her father. She travels back to Brazil every year to see the places of her childhood.

I would like to thank Colonel Friedrich Niko, who has recommended or provided me with good books ever since I first met him.

Thanks to Herwig Art of Art Graphics for the numerous hours we spent in front of his computer, marshaling illustrations through the book's layout.

To my friends, Fred Schlögl, Günther Csitkovits, Werner Fasching, and Felix Jestl, thanks for your untiring support of all my follies, as well as Josef Hettlinger, who departed way too early to the happy hunting grounds.

I express my thanks to Nate Steen from Twin Falls, Idaho, for expertly pondering on archery at the camp fire in the Sawtooth Mountains, Idaho, and Lowell Wolters for doing the cooking.

Thanks to Fritz Massinger and Luis Nowak for reading the manuscript.

My thanks to Austrian editor Rupert Hinterhölzl from Salzburg, for skillfully changing my clumsy scribbling into proper language. To professor Linde Loibl for her useful advice and encouragement. My thanks are also due to my US editor, Jesse Marth.

I express my thanks to the members of the Lockenhaus Longbow Archers, for patiently bearing their chairman's caprices. Thanks also to cowboy and friend, Alex Fuchs, for his support.

I would like to thank my hunting chums, Theo Schett, Karl Hofmeister, and Gottfried Kogler for their invitations and their friendship. I feel extremely grateful to Theo Schett for nicknaming me "The Lazy Hunter" and "Zirben Ghost."

My thanks to Dr. Andreas Gebert for his annual hunting invitations to Neckenmarkt.

I was not always successful but I tried hard to get the best out of the pictures, even though some were of poor quality. I did my best also to give proper credit to all sources.

I would like to apologize for any errors or mistakes which I am certain I made.

Peter O. Stecher, Lockenhaus, 2008
www.legends-in-archery.com

Introduction

Like lots of people of my generation, I loved reading "Cowboy and Indian" stories and watching Hollywood adventure movies throughout my childhood and youth. I was smitten with accounts of travelers' and explorers' experiences. I was fascinated by Errol Flynn playing Robin Hood. Lex Barker or Gordon Scott playing Tarzan were OK, too. They were all brave and intelligent, they knew how to experience real adventures, and they all shot a bow and arrow.

A free, adventurous life in Sherwood Forest or in the African wilderness would have suited my taste. With elegant and effortless grace, these fellas handled their longbows, generally leading a rather tranquil life between their exciting adventures. I could have imagined being a pirate in the Caribbean, a trapper, or a white hunter, like Clark Gable or John Wayne on safari in Africa. I still have and still cherish remnants of these beautiful, albeit unrealistic, dreams, very often to the chagrin of friends and family.

Image 1. The author shooting his beloved longbow.

In the beginning of the 1990s, I started shooting the bow and arrow earnestly. Weapons stores that carried bows and arrows back then mainly had Bear products in their programs—the catalogues often depicted a lean, weather-beaten man with a recurve bow, quiver, plaid shirt, and Borsalino Hat.

Despite the fact that the compound bow was widely used for hunting, and Fred

Bear himself sold many of them, he shot a simple recurve bow. That gave me food for thought and I traded my Jennings compound for a Bear Kodiak recurve, realizing that there was a different form of archery, more native, less logical, and more fulfilling—a form worth preserving.

After reading a translation of Saxton Pope's *Hunting with the Bow and Arrow*, I knew that that was what I had been looking for. Reading Pope's book, I learned a lot about the origins of our sport. By the time I finished the book, I knew I needed a longbow. I got a Ben Pearson "Ol' Ben," and I have only been shooting longbows and wooden arrows from then on, making quivers and arrows according to Pope's descriptions.

My friend Karl Hofmeister recommended *Traditional Bowhunter* magazine and I learned a lot about American archers and bow and arrow literature classics.

Books by Howard Hill, Fred Bear, Robert Hardy, James Duff, Paul Comstock, Bob Swinehart, Bill Negley, Jay Massey, Dan Bertalan, and many other bow and arrow authors were gradually occupying my bookcase. My poor English, which I learned at school many years prior, improved quickly as I read books and magazines only available in English. At first I bought a few classics like the *Legends of the Longbow* series by Glenn St. Charles, which was available as a reprint. But soon I wanted to have original editions, so I gave the reprints to friends who were less weird than I was and replaced them with the more expensive, and rare, albeit marvelous, original editions. Searching secondhand bookshops the world over became mush easier with the help of the Internet.

I am often surprised how little we know and how mistaken we are about the pioneers of archery. Not everyone wants to buy and read a great number of books. I have always wanted to have one book, in German, that presents the legends in archery and provides illustrations, stories, facts and figures—a book that is affordable for everyone interested.

After years of unknowingly doing research, and a phone call to Austrian publisher Didi Vorderegger, I started writing articles on veteran bowmen for the Austrian archery magazine *Bogensport Journal*. This finally resulted in the idea of writing a book.

I knew that the book would never be exhaustive or complete—there are too many details, too many avid archers of past and present that remain unknown to me. But this, perhaps, has made it possible for me to write a more enjoyable book, a book that offers a better overview than a meticulous reference work would have.

For this book there is one aspect that is definitely unfair; I decided to write only about archers of the West. Their stories are well documented and most of the information on them was obtainable without too much effort.

I have, therefore, avoided subject matters I am not that familiar with, such as the Japanese Kyudo, North and South American Native Archery, Asian, African, and ancient bowmen.

I was not interested in describing the bow as a weapon used against men.

I am also well aware that it was unfair not to write about the numerous, excellent tournament and International Archery Federation (FITA) archers. It would have been possible to do research on them by consulting scoring records, but I believe this kind of research would be too boring to present in an enjoyable and enthusiastic way. Anyway, there are top-notch FITA year books documenting the skills and achievements of these archers.

Wherever possible, I indicated my sources. I have also included some original text from primary resources to convey the atmosphere of the old times and provide an authentic portrayal of the archers.

Lots of, but not all, pioneer archers were hunters, too. In recent years, hunting has become a controversial topic for many people, and therefore I avoided writing about hunting scenes and hunting trophies, apart from a few exceptions.

Judged according to today's standards and values, many things done in the old times would not be acceptable today—of course, that is not exclusive to hunting.

Curiously, nobody objects to historical reports on the bow and arrow being used as weapon of war. The widespread interest in war and murder is astounding, but when it comes to hunting, people get upset.

I think a modern hunter intends to lead a more native life style, dominated by nature, making the most of everything it has to offer. Maybe he/she also regards hunting as an opportunity to reject our consumer society, believing that he could live without depending on supermarkets and the meat industry (bowhunters excluded!).

For the hunter, it is not about right or wrong. He has mounted a few trophies on the wall; looking at them, he thinks, "*Well, that was when I met my friends at that place, we were having a good time. What an adventure, we were soaked to the skin, trousers bloodied. The dogs did a good job and afterwards we had a few drinks and ate the liver, which I prepared fresh. And we were joshing about our shooting skills —just like a 100,000 years ago...*"

Those who want to hunt, just do it. Those who don't want to hunt, don't do it. The development of today's traditional archery has always been closely knit with hunting. Bowhunting is certainly one of the fairest hunting forms. Everyone who has tried it will agree.

I am impressed by the archery old-timers' spirit, bravery, and love of adventure. I think one should regard their adventures as some kind of modern heroic saga.

This book is about archery enthusiasts, their tackle, their works, and their lives.

> *For the benefit of the archers I will describe the tackle used on this hunt. All of us had yew bows. Our broadheads were made from saw steel and were 5" long, everything entirely home-made. I was shooting the lightest bow with a pull of 84 pounds. Ken had his old faithful of 103 pounds and Howard was shooting his 108-pound buffalo bow.*
>
> –Walt Wilhelm,"Wild Boars and Bows," August 1936, *Ye Sylvan Archer Magazine*.

Maurice and Will Thompson

Maurice and Will Thompson

Image 2. Will and Maurice Thompson

Wounded and wasted, Maurice, or Morris, as his family called him, finally arrived at his home on the Coosawattee River. Like his home state of Georgia, his uniform was torn, bloody, and burnt.

In 1862, at the age of 17, he had enlisted in the 63rd Regiment of Georgia Volunteers. Like his father, Grigg, and his brother, Will, he fought in the Civil War until 1865.

The war seemed at the Thompson's doorstep and at one point the Union Army burned down bushes, hedges, and trees surrounding the Thompsons' house. Maurice could remember happier days on the Coosawattee. Spending most of their time outdoors, Maurice and Will had gone into the woods and swamps, fishing and hunting birds and rabbits with bow and arrow. They often left their parents' farm on the river for days, camping in the wilderness and enjoying a life only controlled by such basic needs as eating, drinking, and sleeping.

Maurice and Will had a passion that distinguished them from many of their contemporaries—they enjoyed reading books and admired people able to write fascinating stories or poetry. Their interest in literature and their passion for the bow and arrow made the brothers unforgettable.

James Madison Thompson was born on September 9, 1844, in Fairfield, Indiana. He was the fifth child of Grigg Thompson and Diantha Jagger Thompson. Early on, the boy changed his name into Maurice Thompson, pronouncing it "Morris."

His brother Will Thompson was born in Missouri in 1846. In 1855, they finally settled down in Georgia, close to the Coosawattee River, where the two brothers spent an adventurous, happy youth until the beginning of the American Civil War in 1861 and their enlistment in the Confederate Army in 1862. When they came home from war, they found their parents' farm devastated and burned to the ground. They had a hard time making a meager living doing odd jobs.

After the war, the government forbade former Confederate soldiers from using firearms. So they began hunting with bow and arrow again—their boyhood pastime was now almost a necessity. I can easily imagine that the Thompsons were happy about their longbow shooting prowess.

With the little money they had, they bought books, usually reference books on mathematics, engineering, or law. They liked studying their books at night, a habit that became beneficial later on. Maurice took up writing poems and essays, some of which were published in Scott's Monthly.

He learned a lot from studying and soon began to earn money as an engineer and legal counsel. Later on, Maurice traveled to Indiana, where he met a girl and got married. His father-in-law had a firm working for the railroad company and he employed Maurice as Chief Engineer. Will followed his brother to Indiana and started working for the same firm.

In 1873, the two brothers established a law practice. The hard times were over, they became independent and devoted much of their time to the bow and arrow and writing.

Maurice published *The Longbow*, his first article on the bow and arrow, in *Appleton's Journal.* Subsequently, a host of his poems, illustrations, and bow hunting stories were published.

In July 1878, he published his first book, *The Witchery of Archery*, which was comprised of articles on bow hunting that were previously published in *Appleton's Journal*, plus a number of new chapters on shooting technique and archery equipment. There was even one chapter on women in archery. The book was an instant success and sold very well.

Image 3. A prize shot.

In those days, tournament archery was a popular, albeit somewhat elitist, lawn-sport, like tennis. Maurice's book, which focused more on bowhunting, awakened a country-wide interest in this form of hunting. It appealed to the Americans' pioneering spirit and love of challenges.

In 1879, Maurice and Will developed an extensive reference book on tournament archery entitled *How to Train in Archery, Being a Complete Study of the York Round.*

One of their journeys brought the Thompson brothers to Florida, where they were hunting geese and herons on the St. John's River. They discovered and joined a group of Civil war deserters who were bowhunting, too. They spent 37 days on the Kissimmee River, going over Lake Okeechobee and back to the St. John's. They made their arrows from reeds or similar materials; cutting it while still green, they dried and bent the shafts over fire, made the nocks, and fletched the arrows. Even without tools, and in particular special fletching tools, they managed to make 200 arrows per day. As you can imagine, having a good supply of arrows was important to being good at hunting wildfowl. Maurice documented their average number of game killed:

> *My score was ninety-eight shots, seventy-seven arrows lost, sixteen birds killed on the wing – the best score I ever made. Will shot one hundred and twenty-one times, lost forty-six arrows, and killed nineteen birds.*

You could say it was an arrow-consuming sport. However, I would not feel sorry for any arrow lost. Art Young once said that he would like to swap each deer he had killed with a gun for one he had missed with a bow.

There were other reasons why Maurice was smitten with the "Glorious Weapon," as he used to call the English longbow. When he missed a waterbird once, he was still able to shoot a second or third time with the soundless longbow. However, a single gun shot would have frightened away all the gamefowl on the lake.

Will Thompson was a renowned author, too. In 1878, *Forest and Stream* published his article, *Archery Ranges and Bows.* Over the following years, he continued writing essays about the bow and arrow for magazines and newspapers.

The books and deeds of these two bow and arrow pioneers ensured that "archery fever" gripped men like Saxton Pope and Arthur Young. Maurice and Will Thompson will remain unforgettable, they are the fathers of archery and modern bowhunting in North America. *The Witchery of Archery*, available as a reprint, is a wonderful, poetic book, showing the reader the beginnings, the very origin of modern day archery. We cannot add anything at all to Maurice's own words:

Image 4. Stringing the bow.

So long as the moon returns in the heaven, a bent, beautiful bow, so long will the fascination of archery keep hold of the hearts of men.

References:
Maurice Thompson, *The Witchery of Archery*
Saxton Pope, *Hunting with the Bow and Arrow*
T.J. Conrads, *The Traditional Bowhunter's Handbook*
Fred Anderson, *The Traditional Way: The Mystique and Heritage of Archery*

Ishi

Ishi

Image 5. Ishi

Oroville, California, 1911—There are loud barking dogs behind the slaughterhouse at the corral.

It is a cold morning in August when the butcher's son is woken up by the noise. He gets into his trousers and shirt, wondering what this early hubbub is about. When the boy cannot find anything suspicious outside, he goes into the stable at the corral. When his eyes get used to the dark inside, the boy stops dead in his tracks. Huddled in a corner of the stable there is a man—emaciated, naked except for a piece of torn canvas.

The butcher's son had discovered Ishi, the last living member of the Yahi, the last surviving group of the Yana people. He had wrapped himself in a piece of canvas torn from one of the wagons. The frightened boy called his father. The butcher phoned the Sheriff in Oroville and then took the "wild man" with him to the station. The sheriff didn't really know what to do with Ishi, and jailed him at first. Ishi was sick with fear. For years he had believed that white men brought death. The sheriff offered Ishi some food and water, which he rejected even though he was hungry.

Ishi had a small piece of wood in his nose and a deer hide stud in his ear. The sheriff thought Ishi was crazy. It seemed obvious to him that this wild man didn't know a single English word, and that he didn't want to eat or drink.

Soon everyone had learned about the "wild man", and an anthropologist, Professor T.T. Waterman of the University of California, is sent to investigate the case. Waterman wants to communicate with the Native American and brought a word list of various native dialects with him. Ishi didn't understand any of the languages, he didn't recognize a single word. Waterman was about to give up when he knocked on the cot on which Ishi was sitting and said, "*Swimi,*" which means pine. Suddenly Ishi's eyes lit up and he asked Waterman, "*I nu ma Yaki*?" or "Are you a Yahi?" Waterman answered that he was and the fear left Ishi's face.

Ishi was the last Yahi, a descendant of the southernmost tribe of the Yana people. They lived in isolation in a sixty-by-forty-mile area in the foothills of Mount Lassen in Northern California. Since 1840 the Yana had been hunted and almost erased by white settlers. Ishi was the last survivor of this tribe, which once had more than 2,000 members. Ishi's rapid transition from the Stone Age to the relatively modern world of 1911 would contribute a lot to the popularization of archery.

Ishi was taken to San Francisco, to the University of California Museum of Anthropology, where he got a room and was fed and clad. Professor Alfred Louis Kroeber, who was working for the museum, was responsible for Ishi and showing him the modern world. Subsequently, the two men became friends. Soon, the "Big Chief," as Ishi called the professor due to his position at the museum, introduced the Native American to Dr. Saxton T. Pope. Pope was a surgery instructor at the University's medical school, which was situated next to the museum and Ishi's place.

Ishi showed Pope how to make bows and arrows, how to hunt with them, and a lot more about life outdoors. Ishi and Pope spent many hours together working on their archery equipment, shooting, and getting to know each other's language and culture. Later on, when Ishi became ill, Pope did everything he could to he get him healthy. Ishi had lived in such a clean, unspoiled environment, that he had no natural resistance to the diseases of the modern, inhabited world. The Native American called Pope *Ku Wi,* or Medicine Man, and Dr. Pope believed he did so, "*...more, perhaps, because I could perform little sleight of hand tricks, than because of my profession.*

Contrary to what one might expect, Ishi was not very surprised or shocked about the white man's technical inventions. According to Saxton Pope, Ishi regarded the white men as "big children," inventing all kinds of unnecessary toys. He believed they were clever, but not wise. In *Ishi's Medical History,* Pope describes a characteristic situation: Ishi saw a plane in the sky over San Francisco. He asked the surgeon if there were white men in there. Pope said yes. Ishi only shook his head, laughing kindly.

Image 6. Ishi with whitetail buck.

In 1914, the surgeon wanted to make a hunting trip to Ishi's home country. Ishi did not want to go, saying, "*...there are no houses for living, no chairs, no bed, and no food, it is cold and uncomfortable there.*" Finally, Ishi gave in and they started their journey on horseback in May. Ishi had not been riding for quite some time. He shot his last horse before he came in touch with white civilization, as there was little game for hunting.

Dr. Pope, Pope's eleven-year-old son Saxton Jr., Ishi, Waterman, and A.L. Kroeber journeyed to the land of the Yahi. They had a special license, issued by the California Fish and Game Commission, allowing them to shoot "...one item of male game for scientific purposes."

They set up camp along Deer Creek and Mill Creek, enjoying life in the wilderness. Ishi became a "wild man" again, wearing a loincloth, remembering his old way of life outdoors. The other members of the expedition took up many of his habits, but they did not wear loincloth. They only took off their clothes when bathing or swimming. In his home country, Ishi remembered many details of his past. He showed his companions old camp sites used by his people. One day, when they were passing a great rock, Ishi uncovered with his foot the bones of a bear that his people had killed, roasted, and eaten there years ago. Their caravan made a long, thorough excursion through Ishi's land. Maps were drawn, camp sites marked, and caves and other crucial sites where Ishi's people hid from the whites were noted. At the end of May they started their journey home. Apart from the archeological results, invaluable for the white men, Ishi had also benefited from this excursion. He regarded his companions and friends as family and he had enjoyed the trip, in spite of the sorrowful memories connected with his home country. Pope, having a romantic streak, wrote down the following:

> *We swam the streams together, hunted deer and small game, and at night sat under the stars by the camp fire, where in a simple way we talked of old heroes, the worlds above us, and his theories of the life to come in the land of plenty, where the bounding deer and the mighty bear met the hunter with his strong bow and swift arrows.*

Nevertheless, Ishi was happy to leave the land of his fathers. He felt the spirits of the murdered members of his tribe and his family outdoors in the woodlands. Back in San Francisco, he was happy to return to the white man's comfortable life.

In 1915, Ishi and Saxton Pope met Will Compton and Art Young. The four men soon became friends. A year later they were hunting a lot around San Francisco, making bows and arrows, and spending a lot of time together.

Ishi also demonstrated his method of making bows, arrows, and arrowheads for the public. While at the Anthropology Museum, he often made beautiful arrowheads, fashioned from glass cracked off beer bottles. Some of these perfect hunting heads are illustrated in Dr. Pope's work *Yahi Archery*. I bought *The Rarest Works of Saxton Pope*, published in the 1990s and edited by Gene Wensel. The volume contains *Yahi Archery, Ishi's Medical History,* and *A Study of Bows & Arrows.* Anyone interested in Ishi, Native Americans, and the bows and arrows of various other peoples should try to get hold of this work. *A Study of Bows & Arrows* relates Pope's experiences experimenting with bows and arrows from all over the world. He ruined several museum exhibits.

Ishi contracted tuberculosis, maybe through meeting lots of museum visitors. Even though Dr. Pope provided the best medical care, Ishi was fading away. His body was failing rapidly and at the end he was almost unable to eat, consumed with fever. But even during the last days of his life, he was not unhappy. When Pope talked about the bow and arrow, Ishi beamed. He continued working in spite of his disease, fletching shafts, fitting stone heads. When he was too tired to work, he taught Pope various arrow making methods or a new form of bow backing. After months of misery, Ishi suddenly died of a tremendous pulmonary hemorrhage caused by the tuberculosis. Pope was with him. In Ishi's language there was no word for "good bye," he simply said, *"I go, you stay."*

Pope gave Ishi a number of important items on his last journey: fire sticks, one of his bows, five arrows, a small bag of acorn meal, some tobacco, and dried venison. These were cremated with Ishi and the ashes were put in an earthen jar, bearing the inscription, "Ishi, the last Yana Indian, 1916."

After Ishi's death Pope wrote:

> *And so departed the last wild Indian of America. With him the Neolithic epoch terminates. He closes a chapter of history. He looked upon us as sophisticated children— smart, but not wise. We knew many things and much that is false. He knew nature, which is always true. He was essentially kind; he had courage and self-restraint, and though all had been taken from him, there was no bitterness in his heart. His soul was that of a child, his mind that of a philosopher.*

For Saxton Pope, Ishi was family. He mourned for him for a long time, remembering the happy times roaming the woods together. Ishi had taught him everything about the bow and arrow. With this firsthand knowledge, and under William Compton's influence, Saxton Pope and Art Young would write bow and arrow history.

References:
Saxton T. Pope, *Hunting with the Bow and Arrow*
Saxton T. Pope, *Yahi Archery*
Theodora Kroeber, *Ishi in two Worlds*
Gene Wensel, *The Rarest Works of Saxton Pope*

Horace A. Ford

Horace A. Ford

Image 7. Horace Alford Ford

When I think of Horace A. Ford, Saxton Pope's words come to my mind:

> *However, not all temperaments are suited to archery. There must be something within the deeper memories of his inheritance to which the bow appeals. A mere passing fancy will not suffice to make him an archer. It is the unusual person who will overcome the early difficulties and persevere with the bow through love of it.*

–Saxton Pope, *Hunting with the Bow and Arrow*

Ford revolutionized archery. Until today, his shooting style, the results of his detailed studies and his accomplishments with the bow and arrow, has been a serious criterion by which successful shooters are judged. What today's FITA trainers try to teach their shooters is based upon Ford's recommendations. His accurate observations take archery to some kind of art. Horace Alford Ford of Glamorgan, Wales, published the book *Archery: Its Theory and Practice,* which is, together with Sir Roger Ascham's *Toxophilus*, one of the British books that every archer should read and have on his/her bookshelf. Maurice Thompson said about Ford, "...no better Archer ever lived."

The main features of Ford's shooting technique are still a popular criterion for target archers. Even though he had initially developed them for his own needs, Ford's shooting technique is so clear and well reasoned, that it has been easy for other shooters to practice their shooting accordingly and successfully. Ford may be regarded as the father of the point of aim method.

Studying the history of English archery, you will find no archer capable of challenging Ford's title as Great Britain's Greatest Archer.

Ford's career started in Brighton, in 1845. Four years later he won the Champion Medal at the Grand National Meeting at Derby, marking the beginning of an incredible winning streak. In 1857, he scored 1251 points in the Double York Round—a record that would remain unbreakable for the following 72 year, until Dr. E. K. Roberts of Ventura, California broke it in 1929 in Santa Monica, California. Celebrating his score, Dr. Roberts was carried from the field sitting upon a target held by his friends.

Ford's style was reputed to be too awkward and lacked elegance according to the spectators. One lady archer made the following comment, "*Well, I had rather miss in that gentleman's style than hit in Mr. Ford's.*"

In 1859, after he had won his eleventh consecutive Championship, Ford's shooting prowess changed for the worse due to failing health. His shooting had been "overbowed" for too many years. He repeatedly warned other archers of this flaw in his book. Ford struggled for several years, trying to get back to his once masterly shooting skill. Then, in 1867, in Brighton, where Horace Ford had begun his archery career, he won his twelfth and last Championship. In the years after, Great Britain's Greatest Archer still tried to regain his former top-notch form. He participated in tournaments, but to no avail due to injured muscles in his drawing hand.

Horace A. Ford, the gentleman archer, died at his residence in Bath, on June 24, 1880. I highly recommend reading Ford's book. Horace Ford was a scholar and the bow and arrow confided their most mysterious secrets to him

References:

Horace A. Ford, *Archery: It's Theory and Practice*
Robert Hardy, *Longbow*
J. E. Davis, *Ye Sylvan Archer Magazine*

William J. Compton

William J. Compton

Wolf Voice was giving the hint of an appreciative bow towards the white boy. Actually, just his eyelids were giving that hint. The eyes, nestled between deep wrinkles in the weather-beaten face of the old Indian, lit up. The Compton boy had shot three arrows in rapid succession at a mud mound fifteen feet away. The palm of a hand would suffice for covering the group of arrows. Clad in leggings and a breechcloth, without shirt, like the Sioux boys, he lowered the Osage bow. Back in the cloth he still had two arrows with blunt horn-heads. The boy had made his tackle according to the instructions and the bows and arrows of Wolf Voice. He had only changed a minor detail which he thought would improve the bow.

The old man reached for the boy's bow in order to look it over. With both hands Will handed him the bow. The Chief moved it around, screwing up one eye to see whether the bowstring was in the middle between the handle and the limbs. Suddenly, he raised his eyebrows, looking quickly towards Will who was embarrassed and looked at the ground.

"Your bow tips are finer and more slender than those of my bows," Wolf Voice said with the hint of a reproach in his voice. "You will see, the bow is good and fast-shooting now, but it will break soon—presumably, when you want to shoot at a stout stag—you will remember my words." Hesitating and turning red in his face, Will answered, "The wood allowed it and I followed the wood." The boy expected a lengthy sermon about the forefathers of the Sioux, traditions, and how a bow should look like. The old man was looking at the boy for some time; but then he had to laugh so much that all the downward wrinkles in his face moved upwards. He handed the bow back to the boy. "Where will young men's journey go when they listen more to the voice of the wood than to the voice of their elders?"

William John Compton was born in Flint, Michigan, on September 28, 1863. When William was seven years old, his family moved to Norfork, Nebraska. He spent a lot of time with the local Sioux, learning how to make and shoot the bow and arrow. American authors like Cliff Huntington or T.J. Conrads agree that Will Compton was admitted to or adopted by their tribe. W. B. Wescott wrote about Compton, "Much of the quiet wisdom and deep humility which so profoundly affected those who came to know him in later life he accredited to the Indian tutors of his boyhood."

There is not much information available about the time he spent with the Sioux. Anyway, his nickname "Chief" goes back to his Sioux adventures. William J. Compton grew up in the real "Wild West." Will was only 13 when the Battle of Little Big Horn occurred. The young Will Compton was living and working in Nebraska, Wyoming, Montana and Oregon. He loved the solitude of the wilderness, hunting with his Sioux-style bows. By his 20th birthday he had bagged an impressive number of whitetail deer, antelopes, and wapitis. In 1916, Compton wrote a letter on various topics, as well as bow hunting, to a Mr. H. H. McChesney. He wrote, "I will add that I did not know that there was another white man in the world shooting a bow till 1908 or 1909."

In 1894, Will first heard of a bowyer in Forest Grove, Oregon, named Mr. F. S. Barnes. Compton went to Oregon to harvest yew for Barnes and to learn how to make the English longbow. Compton was an eager pupil. In 1913, after Barnes' death, Will packed up 1000 yew staves (or billets) and moved to California. In 1915, Will visited the last of the Yana tribe, Ishi, in San Francisco, where he met Dr. Pope.

In 1915, at the Panama Pacific Exposition in San Francisco, Will met another man while visiting an exhibition of Japanese bows, arrows, and archery equipment. The good-looking young fella was Arthur Young.

Compton introduced Art Young to Pope. The three toxophilites became friends. Following Will's instructions, they made English longbows. Until then, Pope was only familiar with Ishi's native equipment and made bows and arrows with him. After his time at Mr. Barnes', Will was convinced of the efficiency of the English longbows, and he encouraged Pope and Young to use this bow type, too. English archers introduced these bows, which remained unchanged since the Middle Ages, to America. Until after 1900, the English longbow was the only bow used in earnest throughout the Western world.

Pope and Young nicknamed Compton "Chief" when he told them about his involvement with the Sioux. The Chief, Dr. Pope, Young, and Ishi shot and hunted a lot together. After Ishi died in 1916, the remaining trio became serious about hunting American big game. As Dr. Pope phrased it, "Then our serious work began. We found it...a delightful way of hunting."

Image 8. Art Young, the Chief, and Saxton Pope.

Bowhunting was rather unusual in the United States. Bowhunters with their archaic equipment were often ridiculed by rifle hunters. Publications like Maurice Thompson's *The Witchery of Archery*, and later on, Pope's *Hunting with the Bow and Arrow*, a book full of hunting adventures, including big game and grizzlies, laid the foundations and basis of modern bowhunting. Many Americans, fascinated by Thompson's and Pope's stories, took to this native and athletic form of hunting. By this time, the conquest of the West was history. Civilization, big towns with streetcars, and industrialization caused many people at that time to long for unspoiled wilderness and the adventures of the pioneers' times, believed to be lost.

Compton was friends with a number of noted archers of his time. Stanley Spencer, Cassius Styles, Erle Stanley Gardner, and lots of others appreciated his advice and experience. In *Forest and Stream* magazine, Saxton Pope described some of Compton's bows:

> *His favorite bow, noted for its brilliant cast, pulls 65 pounds. It is light enough for small game and heavy enough for large. He calls it "Wolf Voice"—after an old Sioux Chief. Another bow, pulling 80 pounds, which few men can shoot, he calls "Old Horrible." It could drive an arrow through a buffalo.*

Subsequently, Pope and Young went bowhunting throughout America and in Africa.

Compton never became a popular adventurer like Art Young or a writer like Dr. Pope, who wrote that the Chief was a masterful shot, especially accurate when shooting over long distances, also at running or flying game.

Even though he was sociable, Compton was not one for publicity. Being popular and presenting himself to a large crowd of people were not in his nature or his intention. He preferred pleasant get-togethers to big events. His friend Ray Hodgson described him well:

> *Compton never went in for publicity. He quietly went about helping others. He was a grand instructor and an enthralling lecturer. I have always wondered why Will Compton never got his name mentioned as an inspiration to the archery world. Here in the West there never was a man who sold the sport of archery so thoroughly as did Will Compton. Pope, of course, was capable of writing; Young traveled and lectured; but "Chief" Compton started them all. He was the root. We were all his pupils and all of us oldtimers speak of Compton as being responsible for it all.*

On May 16, 1938, at the age of 75, William "Chief" Compton, the last of that great trio, died. He outlived his two younger friends and pupils in archery, Saxton Pope and Arthur Young, by a couple of years.

In 1947, the National Field Archery Association (NFAA) awarded the Compton Medal of Honor for the first time. Ever since, it has been given to outstanding archers and promoters of archery.

Image 9. Art Young and the Chief.

References:
T.J. Conrads, *The Traditional Bowhunter's Handbook*
Saxton Pope, *Hunting with the Bow and Arrow*
Fred Anderson, *The Traditional Way: The Mystique and Heritage of Archery*

Arthur H. Young

Arthur H. Young

A tall, lean man with a prominent nose, slightly protruding ears and light eyes sat in his favorite theater in Detroit. He was young, wore a jacket and a tie and on his right knee there was an elegant, brown Borsalino hat. The theater was well-attended, the piano man was doing his best. Suddenly, the young man grabbed his Borsalino hat, moved forward in his wooden chair, gave up his comfortable slouch, and stared at the screen, enchanted, as if he could not believe his eyes.

Arthur Young, clad like a hunter in the old West, wearing a fringed leather jacket, breeches, and high, laced hunting boots, is stalking through the open country, only a few single trees, and some low bushes providing cover. He is wearing a wide-brimmed, tapered cowboy hat, and on his back, below the right shoulder, attached to a leather strap, there is his quiver.

The hunter is holding a short English longbow in his left hand, moving from bush to bush, cautiously maneuvering away from the camera to the edge of a clearing; he is now crouching behind a bush, an arrow with a big, two-blade hunting head on the bowstring.

The camera swerves to the right, capturing seven Grizzlies, going for a leisurely stroll. Three of them have noticed Art Young; they stop again and again, rise onto their hind legs, looking into the direction of the man. Art adjusts his hat, looking excitedly towards the bears. When they are on level with Young, he looks over his left shoulder, to the cameraman, to find out whether he is also ready. The hunter stands up, the bears stop and stare at him. The first and biggest of the bears lifts himself onto his hind legs, showing not only his impressive height, but also his equally impressive teeth. The hunter knows that this threatening power demonstration might not last long, the grizzly will soon go down on his forelegs, charge at him with a few, quick jumps—attack him. Apart from the cameraman there is no one else, no rifle man as backup.

The man in the suede jacket stands up, draws his bow and shoots. The arrow pierces the heart of the standing bear; the shaft going deep into its chest, only the feathers can be seen. The bear goes down on his forelegs and runs away to the right, the other bears following. The hunter, quick as lightening, nocks the next arrow and pursues the fleeing bears…

Image 10. Art Young in the film *Alaskan Adventures.*

The young man in the theater leaned back in his seat again. He held his hat at its brim, its bottom upwards. You can see the sweatband: "Fred Bear, Michigan" is printed in golden letters on the leather band.

At the theater, Fred Bear had seen *Alaskan Adventures*. He met Arthur Young soon afterwards and became an enthusiastic archer and bowhunter. Fred Bear often talked about the influence this movie had on him and the course of his life. A re-release of the film, titled *Art Young: A Bowhunting Legend,* and produced by Stoney Wolf Productions, is available on VHS—no matter what today's opinion on hunting is, the movie is worth seeing. The grizzly scene is terrifying and shows the spirit of the old bowhunters.

The Alaska expedition lasted two years, the movie shows hunting adventures, as well as some marvelous landscape. I believe, today, nobody would dare to hunt grizzlies with a bow and arrow from the ground. Even with a gun, attempting this could come to a very bad end. Art Young regularly achieved this kind of feat. Dr. Saxton Pope wrote about his friend and companion:

> *Here is no common hunter, no insensate slayer of animals. Here we have a poet afoot—the archaic adventurer in modern game fields; the champion of fair play and clean sport; all that is strong and manly. I take off my hat to Arthur Young.*

Arthur H. Young was born August 17, 1883, in Kelseyville, California. He had an older sister, Orrie, and three younger brothers, Willard, Charlie, and Roy. His father, William Gaylord Young, a Union Army veteran, had moved west in 1881 and settled in Kelseyville, close to Mount Konocti, which the local Native Americans thought to be the home of their gods. William G. Young was a school teacher at the local school and owned a store. Later on, Art, like his brothers and sister, attended San Francisco High School. After his father died he returned home to help run the family business. Art and his brothers found plenty of opportunities for hunting and fishing in the area around Kelseyville. Art soon became a master at the rifle and the pistol. Subsequently, he participated successfully in the national competitions held at the Olympic Club in San Francisco. Another hobby, which became a passion with him, was playing the violin. He practiced a lot and wanted to become a violinist. Later on, when he went on hunting trips with Saxton Pope and "Chief" Compton, he always had a little, cut-down violin with him that he played around the camp fire in the evenings.

Art Young was an outstanding athlete, with the talent and body to accomplish most challenges, no matter what kind of sport he was playing. He was, for example, such an excellent swimmer that he thought about taking part in the Olympic Games.

When the family business in Kelseyville was doing well enough without him, Art moved back to San Francisco and started working for the *San Francisco Call* newspaper. He stayed there for 14 years, working in the distribution center, presumably, as a forwarding agent.

In San Francisco, at the Panama Pacific Exposition, fate brought two men together. Art, while visiting an exhibition of Japanese bows and arrows, met Will "Chief" Compton. The two started talking and soon became good friends. Will introduced his new friend to two other toxophilites, Ishi, the last of the Yana tribe, and Dr. Saxton Pope.

The archers began making English longbows from yew. According to Dr. Pope, the "Chief" had brought "...an unlimited supply of yew." Compton taught his friends how to shoot the longbow. Together, they were hunting large amounts of small game in California.

Art Young also became a master at target archery. In the 1920s he won numerous Californian competitions. His contemporaries described him as the epitome of a fine sportsman and gentleman. He did not drink, smoke, or swear, as Mr. Leonard K. Osberg of Detroit, Michigan, stated in the *Alaska Bowmen* magazine. In the 1930s, Mr. Osberg wrote an article about Young, whom he had known personally.

Once Osberg was throwing clay pigeons for Young, Art hit five out of six clay targets in mid-air. Mr. Osberg also did not attribute Art's hunting exploits to sheer luck, but to outstanding skills. Osberg remembered a special episode: Art was hunting moose in Quebec, Canada, with five arrows and his bow. He came back with four arrows and a moose. Standing on a rocking canoe, he had hit the moose bull from 55 yards, right in the heart. Episodes like this one should give a clear picture of Art's prowess as an archer.

In the early 1920s, Art began making English longbows from Osage orange. He obtained this wood from Mr. E. F. Pope of Woodville, Texas. Osage was the bow wood of the Native Americans. Art realized that, unlike yew bows, Osage bows were less susceptible to breaking and more resistant to variations in temperature. Due to the durability of Osage, Art mainly made "shorter" English bows. When hunting, it was a lot easier to handle these shorter bows than the 70 to 72-inch long bows. Like Saxton Pope, Art designed and manufactured all his archery equipment himself. Hunting heads were made from slotted target points with a blade inserted and soldered into a homemade ferrule. Pope preferred simple, deltoid broadheads. Young designed his own broadhead.

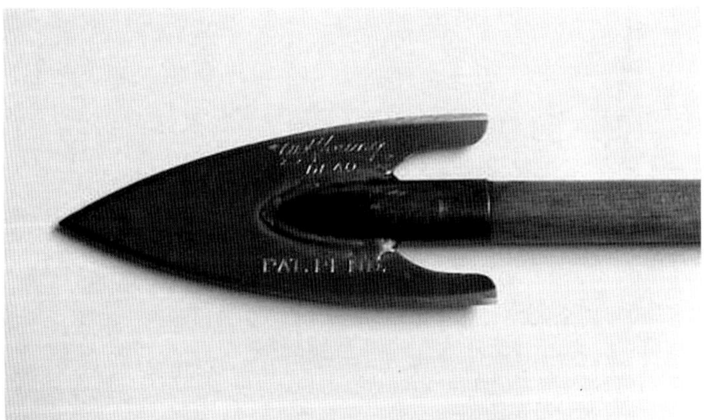

Image 11. Replica of an Art Young head.

At first, even Pope and Young were skeptical of the efficiency of broadheads for hunting big game. For their first hunt on whitetails they used arrows coated with strychnine. When they saw that the arrows, in the majority of the cases, penetrated the animals completely, they began to trust the "killing power" of their feathered shafts. They bagged small game, but also American big game, like whitetail deer, elk, black bear, grizzly, and puma with their bows. Saxton Pope and Art wanted to up the ante by proving the longbow could kill any wild animal in the world.

Image 12. Assyrian relief, from Pope's *The Adventurous Bowmen.*

Dr. Pope discovered men hunting lions with bow and arrow on an Assyrian relief. Thirst for adventure and the desire to popularize bowhunting as socially acceptable gave them the idea to hunt lions in Africa. In Steward Edward White's book, *Lions in the Path*, published in 1926, one finds a beautiful and amusing description of Pope and Young preparing for their African journey in 1925. White accompanied the two archers on their trip to Africa. Here follows an excerpt that I don't want to withhold from you:

> *That was after we actually began to get ready and our friends had begun to josh us with jeering hopes that the lion would at least spit out a wishbone to be sent home as a souvenir. I knew the conditions to be met in the wilder sort of African travel; but we were totally at sea as to what we might need in the way of archery tackle. Would we loose an arrow a day or a dozen? Would our bows stand up under the climate, and would we need to camouflage them? Would strings wear well, or would we have to amend the old proverb about two strings to your bow and make it six? We did not know.*
>
> *So we decided to play safe. The better part of a winter's leisure moments were spent in the preparation of tackle. Our families at first had deprecated the whole idea—"deprecated" is a mild word—but later became more reconciled. Our departure would mean a cessation of shavings on the library floor, sawdust in the living-room rug, glue at disconcerting places, and clinging feather bits wherever a black skirt or coat might tarry the moment. For we made us six bows of yew and of osage apiece, a hundred and fifty arrows and a dozen bow strings Furthermore, we prepared two thousand shafts; we found a man who would and did make as many steel broad-head points; we split and partially trimmed six thousand turkey feathers, and we laid the materials to assemble these components. We might have gone even further had not one of us been statistically minded enough to do some computation.*

"Here," said he, "how long are we going to be in Africa, anyway?"

"Six or seven months," quoth we; "you know that."

"Well, as near as I can make out, we're going to spend all our time there in camp making arrows. Figure it out for yourselves." We did so. We quit. But one day came Young, bearing rather shamefacedly a strange fearsome thing. It looked like a cross between a spear and a butcher knife. It was six inches or more long, shaped like an arrowhead and whetted to a razor edge.

"What's that thing?" we begged to know.

"That?" said he, staring at it as though he saw it for the first time. "That. Why, that's a rhino head."

We pointed out that we were just going to get some shooting where game is very plenty, not to do any stunts; that the big fellows ... .

"It might come handy," he countered vaguely.

He went away. Later, it developed, he made six of the things. What is worse, he infected Doc, who also made six. I did not I am without rhino arrows. But then, as I said, I am not an archer; I only shot the bow and arrow a little.

–Steward E. White, *Lions in the Path*

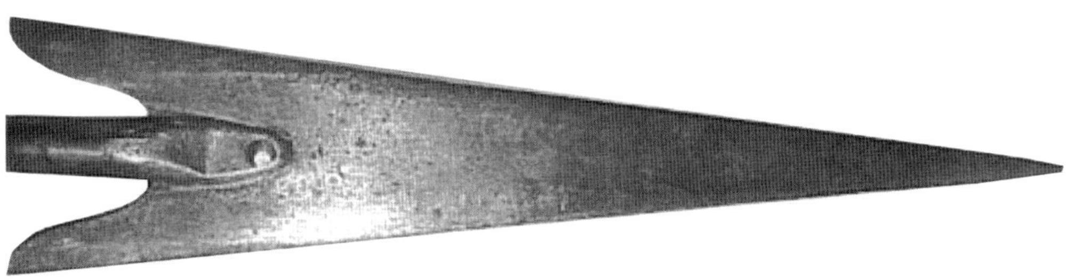

Image 13. Saxton Pope's "Rhino Head," 1925, was over 7 inches long.

Generally, Steward Edward White was a rifle hunter, but at times he also hunted with the bow and arrow. Pope wrote about their adventure in his book *The Adventurous Bowmen*. You get quite a clear picture of the safari, as the journey was described by two different authors and participants. During the journey, Art was corresponding with E. F. Pope, the previously mentioned bowyer and Osage supplier from Woodville, Texas. Mr. Pope (no relation to Saxton T. Pope) published some of these letters in the magazine *American Bowman-Review* in 1937. I'm quoting an excerpt from one of these letters. Reading it, you will catch a very private glimpse of

Young. In his characteristic and familiar thoughts, enthusiastic bowmen, hunters, and bowyers recognize their own, almost child-like passion:

June 25th, 1925
At camp, 250 miles from Nairobi.

My dear Pope:

I have for a long time going to write you—and for than one good reason. I have just finished some practice, throwing the heavy spear, such as used in Africa by the natives—and my usual evening, or "before dinner" bath.

Now, back to the first chapter. I have been wishing to tell you about the other half of the stave you sent me, and a part from which you made your Royal Hunting Bow.

The last I wrote you about this piece of wood was not very promising. When it came from the dryer, it was warped in more than one place, and in more than one direction. I thought I had an idea. I am crank on a bow that lines up. I didn't want this bow crooked as it was. I got out my blow torch, put the bow in the vice, then turned the heat on the place desirous of a correction I slightly scorched the wood in some places, which gave it a most wonderful bronzed golden color. I finished the bow, pulling somewhere in the nineties. I have never had a pair of scales to weigh it. Length 5 feet 4 inches. The upper limb has a little cast, due mostly to the curve it took before it went into the dryer, while I was testing it. Let me say I also have a Royal Hunting Bow in this one.

When I came here it was unnamed. I decided or rather vowed I'd kill an African Lion with it, then inscribe the name with his own blood. This I did and now the name "SIMBA (lion) BLOOD" is written on it, and the bloody name is protected by a goodly supply of varnish.

So I hope some day to show you this good bow, with which I have done most of my hunting and shooting here and with the lion's own blood which this bow killed, furnishing the ink for the name.

My other good bow "ALASKA BROWN," which I have used and liked so much, and which went through two seasons with me in Alaska—also with which I have killed two lions here besides other game—I have not used for some time. It seems not strong enough for me. It is 5 feet 4 1/2 inches long, but by cutting an inch off each end, it would transform it from 80 lbs., which it now registers, to well into the nineties, or possibly over the 100 mark.

I don't at least now, intend to cut it shorter. It was my first Osage—which you sent me—and I like to let my sentimental desires rule. Then too, I will not always be so strong as I am now, and hope to shot this bow, when it will be difficult for me to pull it—due to old age.

We left New York on Feb. 22nd. Just one month later to the day—we landed in Mombassa, Africa. About ten days later we were in camp and Doc and I landed our first lion.

The unheard of thing happened...

Art Young was the first white man to take a lion with bow and arrow.

In 1926, Young participated in George P. Putnam's expedition to Greenland on the *Morrissey*, captained by Bob Bartlett, who had been to the North Pole with Admiral Peary in 1909. Young took both walrus and polar bear during the Greenland voyage, which was well documented by David Putnam's *David Goes to Greenland.* David Binney Putnam was the 13-year-old son of publisher George G. Putnam.

Image 14. Arthur Young, the gentleman fighting with lions.

Image 15. Art Young at the Jones Sound, Ellesmere Land.

One of Young's friends was Sasha "Tiger Man" Siemel, who was cut from the same cloth. If we believe what Young's contemporaries said about him, he had almost saint-like qualities. He did not drink or smoke, he did not swear, and he had high moral and ethical values. He was an athlete and extraordinary archer.

Arthur H. Young died on February 26, 1935, at the age of 51, from peritonitis following a ruptured appendix.

References:

Saxton Pope, *Hunting with the Bow and Arrow*

Saxton Pope, *Adventurous Bowmen*

David Putnam, *David Goes to Greenland*

Steward Edward White, *Lions in the Path*

T.J. Conrads, *The Traditional Bowhunter's Handbook*

Fred Anderson, *The Traditional Way: The Mystique and Heritage of Archery*

Cliff Huntington's collected articles, which he has kindly provided. Cliff is a true archery historian and expert.

Saxton T. Pope

Saxton T. Pope

Image 16. Arthur Young and Saxton Pope.

Maurice and William Thompson had a tremendous influence on bowmen and above all on bowhunters. As far as I know, they were the first ones to go public with their passion for bowhunting and support the acceptance of the bow and arrow as a serious hunting weapon. Lots of classical experts, such as Horace A. Ford and Arthur W. Lambert, who wrote books on archery, were pure target archers.

However, Saxton T. Pope's works contributed significantly to the development of today's bowhunting tradition in the United States, and consequently, today's European archery tradition. He continued what the Thompsons had started. Dr. Pope was a scientist and adventurer. He knew how to convey to readers his romantic love of the free, outdoors life and how to enjoy it with fine hunting companions and that glorious weapon, the longbow. I have learned that even non-hunters cannot escape from the magic of Saxton Pope's writing. They usually find a new, different attitude towards the bow and arrow and bowhunting and feel a new freedom.

Saxton T. Pope's *Hunting with the Bow and Arrow* should be found on every bookcase. First published in 1923 by Putnam, it is a romantic, but also informative, illustrated standard of bow and arrow literature. In 1974, Fred Bear took an interest in the book and re-published it. It is still available as a reprint and the original is much harder to come by (and pricey, at about $1,000). In 1985, Herr Quint, owner of the German archery shop, Robin Sport, recognized the value of this book and translated it into German. Although I could stumble through the English version, I was very happy when I could read this wonderful work in my mother tongue. That, I am sure, contributed to my later passion for the bow and arrow, for the hunting tradition, and for reading old hunting and adventure stories.

In addition to *Hunting with the Bow and Arrow,* some of his other publications included: *Yahi Archery* (1918), *The Medical History of Ishi* (1920), and *A Study in Bows and Arrows* (1923). Thanks to Pope, a meticulous chronicler, it is easy to follow the trails of the archery pioneers, at least on paper.

Pope's work captured the dramatic story of Ishi, the last of the Yana tribe, and the friendship between Chief Will Compton, Ishi, Art Young, and Dr. Pope, is known, at least in part, to most of today's shooters. Pope fondly describes the making of his bowhunting equipment in great detail. Saxton Pope and Art Young's hunting trips are legendary in archery history. According to modern hunting criteria, some of their deeds are not up-to-date from an ethical point of view, such as shooting game from a minimum distance of 85 yards. Well, as Pope put it, they either hit the game and the hunters went home with their quarry, or they completely missed it.

One should not forget that in the 1920s there were, worldwide, hardly any laws or ethical guidelines regarding bowhunting. Even in the United States, the bowhunting nation par excellence, hunting with the bow and arrow was neither acceptable nor common.

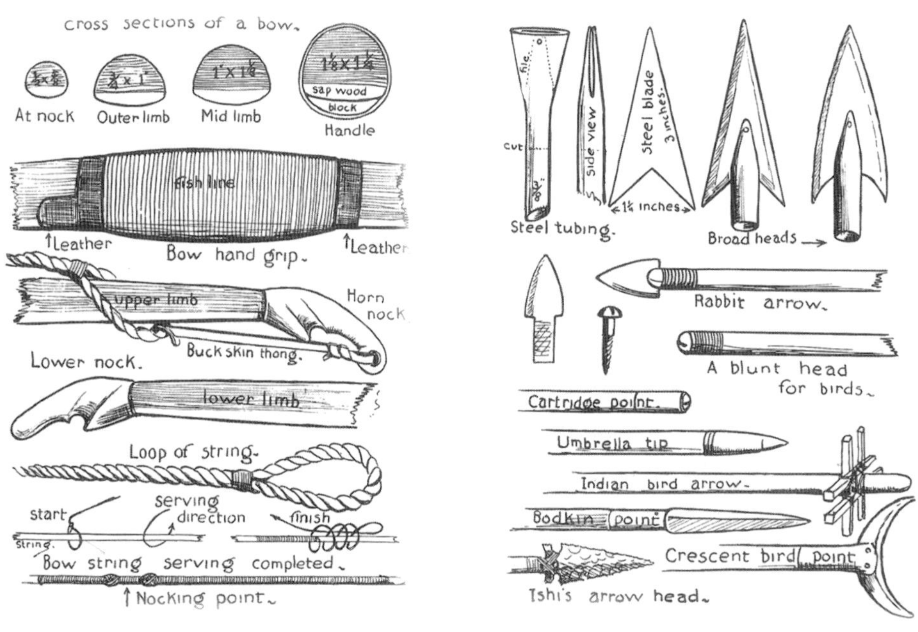

17. Illustrations from *Hunting with the Bow and Arrow.*

Rifle hunters were suspicious of archers with their "toy bows" and refused to consider the bow a serious hunting weapon. The pioneers of our sport, above all Pope and Young, re-introduced the bow, worldwide, as an effective hunting weapon. Subsequently, men like Fred Bear and Howard Hill were gripped by that classic archery fever. Pope, who had been influenced by the Thompson brothers' publications, became an ardent advocate of the English longbow, realizing how effectively its long bow limbs threw a heavy hunting arrow. He benefited from an almost unlimited supply of Will Compton's yew. Pope made a special kind of shooting machine for testing bows and arrows, excluding the influence of the individual archer.

At that time, bow equipment was only designed for target shooting. These were light English longbows that shot light arrows with 3-4" fletching. Pope and Young needed sturdy and safe hunting tackle, which they crafted and partially designed themselves.

Whereas Arthur H. Young was an exceptionally talented sportsman, Saxton T. Pope was a scientific, romantic man that experimented tirelessly. Young did not publish any books, but from time to time he wrote articles for hunting magazines such as *Field & Stream* and *The American Rifleman* or for J. E. Davis' monthly bow magazine, *Ye Sylvan Archer*. Certainly, Young was the better archer, and an excellent rifle and pistol shooter, too.

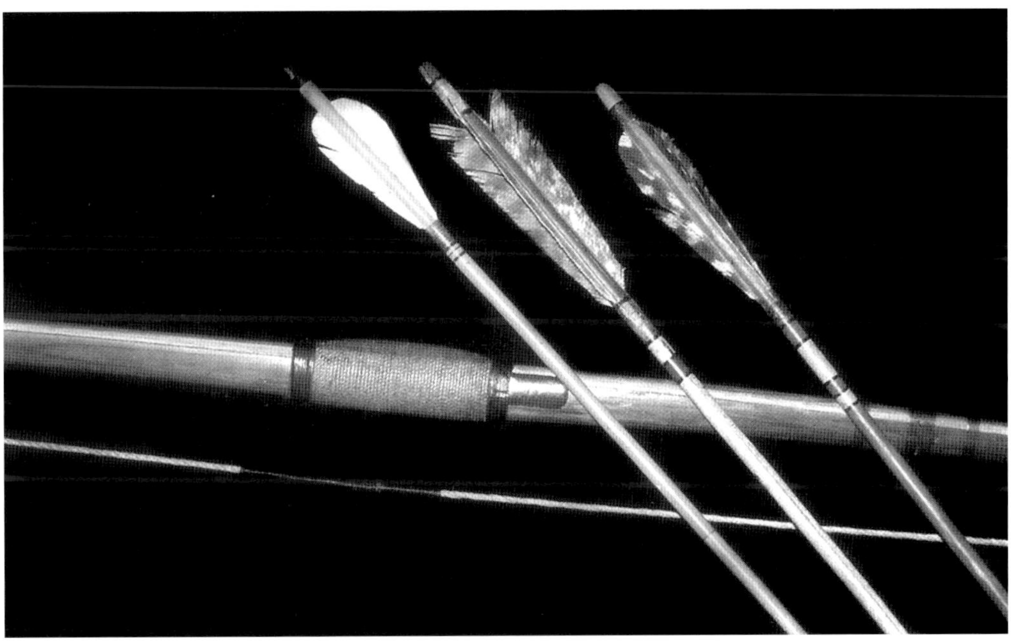

Image 18. English longbow and arrows, Pope's weaponry.

Saxton Temple Pope was born on September 4, 1875, in Fort Stockton, Texas. In 1899, he settled down in Watsonville, California, close to San Francisco, and became an instructor in surgery at the University of Berkely.

Image 19. Different tackle, same target.

Saxton's father, Benjamin Franklin Pope, was an army surgeon. The family moved from town to town throughout the country, depending on where Dr. Pope's army garrison was stationed.

Saxton grew up with soldiers, Native Americans, trappers, hunters, and cowboys. Their "educative" influence may indicate his later passion for hunting, shooting, fishing, and the independent life in the wilderness.

Despite his adventurous youth, he graduated in 1899 with honors and a degree in medicine from the University of California. After his internship, he moved to Monterey, a small town outside of San Francisco, set up a practice there and married Dr. Emma Wightman. They had four children: Saxton Jr., Elizabeth, Virginia, and Willard Lee. For twelve years Pope worked in his practice, then he became a surgery instructor at the University of California medical school. Later on, Saxton became Assistant Professor and then Clinical Professor of Surgery.

Image 20. Pope studying and analyzing museum bows.

Even though Pope was intensively training hospital units during World War I, he still found enough time to publish 32 scientific works.

At the same time, Saxton Pope met Ishi, who was living next to the medical school in the Museum of Anthropology. Ishi called him "Popey" and "Medicine Man." The two men went on adventurous hunting excursions in the surrounding country and Dr. Pope became Ishi's close friend and physician. The Popes often invited Ishi for dinner—Virginia, Pope's daughter, described him as a very polite and kind guest. In accordance with Yana culture, Ishi avoided looking at or talking to Mrs. Pope or other women when he was at their house.

In 1915, Saxton Pope met Chief Compton and Art Young. The three archery enthusiasts and Ishi became friends and spent their leisure time manufacturing bows and archery tackle. They shot at the university's archery range and hunted big and small game in Humboldt County, North California.

As long as they lived, Pope, Young, and Compton were smitten with the bow. Saxton Pope and Art Young were hunted in Northern California for many years, bagging elk, whitetail, black bear, and mountain lions. Soon, they made plans to realize their long-cherished dream—hunting grizzly bears with bow and arrow. Here is a quote from Pope's *Hunting with the Bow and Arrow*, describing what grizzly hunting was like:

> *The very idea of shooting grizzly bears with the bow and arrow strikes most people as so absurd that they laugh at the mention of it. The mental picture of the puny little archery implements of their childhood opposed to that of the largest and most fearsome beast of the Western world, produces merriment and incredulity.*

In 1919, they obtained a license for hunting a limited number of bears in Yellowstone National Park. After killing them, they were to serve as specimens in the California Academy of Sciences Museum. They started the following May, with Ned Frost, a noted grizzly expert from Cody, Wyoming. The party consisted of Art Cunningham, the cook; Pope; Young; Frost; Saxton Pope's brother, G.D. Pope; and Judge Henry Hulbert, their photographer. Every bowhunter had brought along two longbows and a gross of arrows (144). Pope described the equipment as "... the finest assembly of bows and arrows since the battle of Crecy." Saxton Pope used two, 75-pounders, Old Horrible, his favorite, and Bear Slayer, a fine-grained but crooked yew bow, with which he had killed his first black bear in California. Young had a new 85-pounder and his reliable, 75-pound Old Grizzly with him.

Image 21. Ned Frost, grizzly expert from Cody, Wyoming.

Soon they realized that it was not at all easy to find grizzly bears that spring. Time was passing quickly and sooner or later some of the participants would be compelled to go home to dedicate themselves to such mundane things as their jobs. Ned Frost accompanied Pope and Young to a new camp and supplied them with provisions, before he, too, had to go back to Cody, where other hunters where waiting for him. After a couple of days, Art and Saxton spotted a magnificent bear and called it Monarch of the Mountains. They formed a blind above a grizzly pass.

About an hour before midnight, when the moon was at its fullest, the hunters were waiting for the bear. After a couple of hours a strong, female bear with her two cubs came into their ambush. Pope and Young decided that this was the right group for the museum. Yes, times were different back then. When the grizzlies came within range, Pope signalled and the two men shot their broadheads. Each of them hit a cub. The furious female bear tried to find the perpetrators of this act of hostility, discovered the hunters, and immediately proceeded to attack. At that very critical moment for Pope and Young, the Monarch of the Mountains appeared. There were four grizzlies in front of the hunters and all of them had very good reasons for being in a bad mood. Pope signalled Young to shoot Monarch, while he aimed at the heart of the assaulting female.

It gives me the creeps when I imagine confronting one single bear that's in a good mood and unaware of me and my bow and arrow. So I can't begin to fathom fighting several assaulting bears without the help of a backup gunmen.

I do not want to administer too many gory details, so to make a long story short, the grizzlies were killed. The shooters accomplished the feat with an English longbow and broadheads. Those appreciating adventures of this kind should read Pope's accounts.

The Adventurous Bowmen, an absolutely fascinating book published by G. Putnam's & Sons in 1926, is especially interesting because Pope and Young's adventures bring them to a completely new territory—Africa, where they hunted lions with the longbow.

Just reading about the preparations for that trip can send avid archers into rapture. Each of the archers on that trek made more than 1,000 arrows during their journey. I would have loved to hear their conversations. Reading their accounts, one realizes that bowhunters back then did not have any information on what kind of tackle or what hunting technique thcy would need.

Pope came up with the idea for the trip after seeing lion hunts with bow and arrow on Assyrian and Egyptian reliefs. I think by now we know Pope and Young so well that it is clear they wanted to experience that challenge.

Image 22. Dr. Pope and the longbow, after bagging a bear.

The hunters arrived in Mombasa on April 7, 1925, then they continued their journey to Tanganjika.

The professional white hunters on this trip, the bowhunter's "life insurance," were Steward Edward White and Leslie Simson—considered legendary big game hunters even by today's insiders. For lovers of books and lovers of truth, it is very interesting to note that these adventures were also described from the rifle hunter's point of view in Steward E. White's *Lions in the Path* (published by Doubleday, Page & Company in 1926).

White and Simson both appreciated the bow as an archaic hunting weapon, but hey were actually rifle hunters and game photographers. Several times, Pope and Young had to be rescued by the hunters' guns, and curiously, the archers were not able to take enough game to feed the camp. And there was an abundant supply of game that would be unimaginable today. White attributes the "failure" of the bow hunters, the same hunters who had taken an impressive amount of game, from whitetail to grizzly in America, to the extreme alertness and wariness of the African game. Accordingly, the herds, always endangered by the ever-present lions, leopards, and hyenas, are extremely careful, and very often did not allow the bow hunters to get closer than 300 meters.

At that time, safaris were a rather prestigious event. They mainly took place in Kenya, close to Nairobi, and a well-organized hunting tourism market had already developed. White hunters, like Phillip Percival, who later hunted with Ernest Hemingway, were living legends, and had an adventurous, but often very short, life.

Pope and Young didn't plan a luxury safari with every last detail organized. They set up camp in Tanganjika, far away from known hunting areas. The safari was planned for four months. They wanted to hunt lions, not just shoot them.

Back then, and even today, the chosen hunting method makes the difference. Nine out of ten lions, which so-called "great hunters" present to highly-impressed friends in their trophy rooms, have been taken with the help of a rather unsportsmanlike method. The hunting tourist and the professional hunter wait in a *boma*, a hiding place made of strong branches and thorns. The lion is enticed by live bait or a carcass and shot from the safety of the boma.

That's not what the bowhunters wanted. They wanted to hunt the lion in the long grass, in the veld. This method is a great deal more dangerous and crazier, but a lot fairer. Highly alert and extremely strong, the lion, just as any other predator, out matches the bowhunter. An arrow cannot stop an attacking predator. Even rifle hunters have lost their lives in spite of their very effective weapons.

Pope and Young had to be saved several times by the riflemen. The cats of prey, even though fatally wounded, attacked the bowhunters at short bow range. They all came to the conclusion that the bow was not the ideal weapon for hunting big cats. This conclusion led to a different hunting method. Pope, who had admired the reliefs showing lion hunters hunting from a chariot, replaced the ancient vehicle with an automobile. I think it was a Ford Model T (1926).

Hunting from a car was not in line with hunting etiquette, and so the car was only used for inconspicuously bringing the bowhunters closer to the game. The game did not link the automobile with human beings or any imminent danger. They might have regarded it as some close relative of the rhino. They got as close to the lion as possible while remaining inconspicuous. The hunters got off, stalking the animal until they were in bow range. Some lions were bagged with this method, however always under the protection of rifles. Soon it became clear that even this method posed some dangers. On the bumpy ground, the car was not able to go faster than angry running lions. Consequently, this led to some very dangerous situations. I want to describe one of them. A lioness, shot at with a bow and arrow gave chase to the hurriedly fleeing Dr. Pope. Completely exhausted, he finally arrived at the automobile, which was just driving away. He jumped onto the back of the vehicle, desperately clinging to its tailgate.

Image 23. Art Young with his royal quarry in Africa.

The lioness had almost caught up with the automobile and the struggling Pope. Young, Pope's backup man, was not able to aim properly with his rifle due to the bumpy ground, and only hit the animal on his third shot—the very moment before the lioness would have helped Pope enter the happy hunting grounds. After this adventure, the hunters always had a life-sized dummy made from stuffed clothes in their automobile. They threw it out of the auto whenever a lion was seriously following them. The furious cats of prey were occupied with tearing the dummy to tatters, while the hunters were able to escape in their automobile.

During that safari, there were countless other episodes worth mentioning, but I do not want to summarize them all here. My intent is only to that there is a lot of exciting, classic bow literature out there.

Soon after returning from their safari, our bowmen's ways parted dramatically. Saxton T. Pope died of pneumonia in 1926 and in 1935, Arthur H. Young died of a ruptured appendix. Ishi had already succumbed to tuberculosis in 1916. Chief Will Compton survived all of them, passing away in 1938 at the age of 75.

Saxton Pope's accounts and works were always realistic, very detailed, and unpretentiously written. They were never lurid and he never wrote to show off. He was an absolutely respectable reporter, a scientist who represented the true spirit of our sport like nobody else.

Image 24. The "modern" hunting chariot.

Image 25. "... a bent, beautiful bow..."

References:
Saxton Pope, *Hunting with the Bow and Arrow*
Saxton Pope, *Adventurous Bowmen*
Steward Edward White, *Lions in the Path*
T.J. Conrads, *The Traditional Bowhunter's Handbook*
Gene Wensels, *The Rarest Works of Saxton Pope*
J.E. Davis, *Ye Sylvan Archer* magazine

Walt and Ken Wilhelm

Walt and Ken Wilhelm

Image 26. Walter and Kenneth Wilhelm with Howard Hill.

The Wilhelm brothers were unique archers. In Southern California, legendary American archers, including Perry Mason author, Erle Stanley Gardner; the one-legged, Nubbie Pate; Howard Hill; Cassius Styles, the flying ace downed over France during WWI; Jack Willard; Curtis Hill and his brother Ed; George Brommers; Jim "Osage" Murphy; and Walt and Ken Wilhelm met regularly in the desert for the fun of shooting the bow and arrow and to cherish the long-lasting friendship of their group. Walt Wilhelm described their group as "a great gang of sportsmen." Their conversations were usually characterized by their down-to-earth humor and encouraging one another to attempt even bolder bow and arrow feats. No one was able to escape the sarcasm of George Brommers who wrote for *Ye Sylvan Archer* magazine. (In 1994, The Derrydale Press published a series of *Ye Sylvan Archer* back issues as part of the *Legends of the Longbow* series.) Reading issues of this magazine, one will get a clear picture of the spirit of that time and those archers. It is really good reading material.

In the desert, they set up field ranges, but the archers would shoot at anything for fun. There were unlimited small game to hunt—rabbits, wildfowl, and wildcats—they bagged everything. Other activities and field tests included flight-shooting, shooting from moving automobiles, and tying hams in trees to check the arrow penetration of their broadheads. There are movie shorts of Ken and Walt shooting the bow and arrow on www.tradgang.com

Image 27. One of many bold trick shots.

Walter Sherman Wilhelm was born February 27, 1893, in Trenton, Missouri. His brother Kenneth was born on June 8, 1902, in Mackay, Idaho. The Wilhelms lived in Idaho among the Blackfoot until 1908. Later the family moved to Nevada, where they had close contact with the Pajute and Shoshone Native Americans. From what I've learned about the family, I think it's safe to say the Wilhelms were not much for settling down. I think that's what they called pioneering spirit back then.

In 1910, Walt and his brother Ken were in the California desert, close to Yermo. It wasn't until 1925, however, that Walter and Kenneth took up shooting the bow and arrow. By 1928, they had become well-known archers and bowhunters all along the West Coast. Soon the archers would meet other bowmen, among them were Will "Chief" Compton. Due to their passion for archery, maybe also because Compton had close ties with Native Americans, the three men became friends. Just like the Chief, the Wilhelms were always making bows, going all over the country to look for wood. They cut yew, osage, hickory, and sometimes rather unusual varieties like palma brava and mesquite. They believed they made some of their best bows from juniper. They went all the way to Mount Charleston, a traditional bow wood cutting ground of the Native Americans near Las Vegas, Nevada, to cut juniper. The Wilhelm brothers found that burying the green staves in the hot desert sand was the best way to dry bow wood. This method also reduced the time needed for drying. They split and planed arrow billets from cedar railroad ties and both preferred wild bird feathers, like eagle, hawk, and crow, for fletching. Walt once said, "It seems like wild bird feathers fitted hunting and the game better."

Walt Wilhelm is credited with being the first to have used spiral fletching on his arrows.

Speaking of arrows, over the years I've uncovered some instructive insights. I used to collect old hunting heads for a while and so I came across a few arrows from the '40s, '50s, and '60s. I really enjoy looking at these old arrows because when I see work of the great fletcher Hugh Rich (c. 1950), it seems he thought that a drop of glue was needed in the same place where I think it's necessary. When I discover the fine scratches of a knife on the shaft, I know that the old fletcher was as angry as I get when I cut into the shaft when tapering the feathers, thereby producing a potential breakage point.

Image 28. Ken, using pins for fletching.

It is a pleasure for me to look at fine, perfect arrows, especially those that I have received from friends over the years. I have excellent specimens from Jeff Challacombe, the bowyer of Queensland, Australia; Nate Steen, the "Sunset-Hill" bowyer of Twin Falls, Idaho; Theo Schett and Pep Altenberger of Stuhlfelden and Salzburg, Austria; Karl Hofmeister, the bowhunter from Styria, Austria; Fritz Massinger of Waidring, Austria; and Colonel Fritz Niko of Burgenland, Austria. Good arrows are easily recognized —poor ones, too.

Even today, it is not possible to make arrows with machines. Except for the development of fletching apparatus and milling machines, arrows are still made as they were in Saxton Pope's day. On 3D tourneys you can often see arrows that are carelessly made or without the appropriate know-how. Common symptoms are misplaced vanes, disregard for the direction of the wood's grain, askew nocks, and arrows that shoot at their full length of 32" even though the draw length is only 26".

Looking at my vintage arrows from Pearson, Bear, or small manufacturers, I usually discover the following: the quality of the wood is excellent. From 1930 to 1980 cedar shafts were the norm. The fine-grained wood can make arrows that are absolutely straight. The fletching was totally accurate; the cresting, due to the perfectly straight shafts, precise; the nocks were perfect. The quills of the feathers on many old arrows were usually white on the sides and painted the color of the crown-dips in the front where they are tapered. I think that cedar and good-quality sitka spruce make the best arrows. I have seen so many arrows made from pine and regional spruce break along their grain upon impacting 3D targets, that I no longer use them in the quality they are currently offered.

As the old saying goes: reasonably good results can be achieved with a poor bow and good arrows, but with an excellent bow and poor arrows, even the best archer will not hit the target. One should always bear that in mind when making arrows.

Well, now back to Walt and Ken. The Wilhelm boys had a lot of fun teaching neophytes how to shoot the bow and arrow. Actor Roy Rogers, for example, was one of their students.

In the 1930s, Ken took up flight shooting. Ken was not of tall stature, but a very strong man. He could shoot a 125-pound Osage bow over 550 yards, bare fingered! He went to a lot of flight events. In 1939, in Amarillo, Texas, his best foot-bow shot was 896 yards, a world record. With the hand bow he shot 597 yards and seven inches. On October 1, 1938, he shot 758 yards with a 250-pound foot bow. These were amazing distances when you think of the materials used for building bows in those days.

During the 1930s, Walt was regularly writing bow and arrow stories. Ken and Walt also performed as trick shooters in lots of shows. Hollywood, always looking for new forms of entertainment, discovered Ken and Walt, whose down-to-earth humor and their hair-raising stunts were perfect for the film industry.

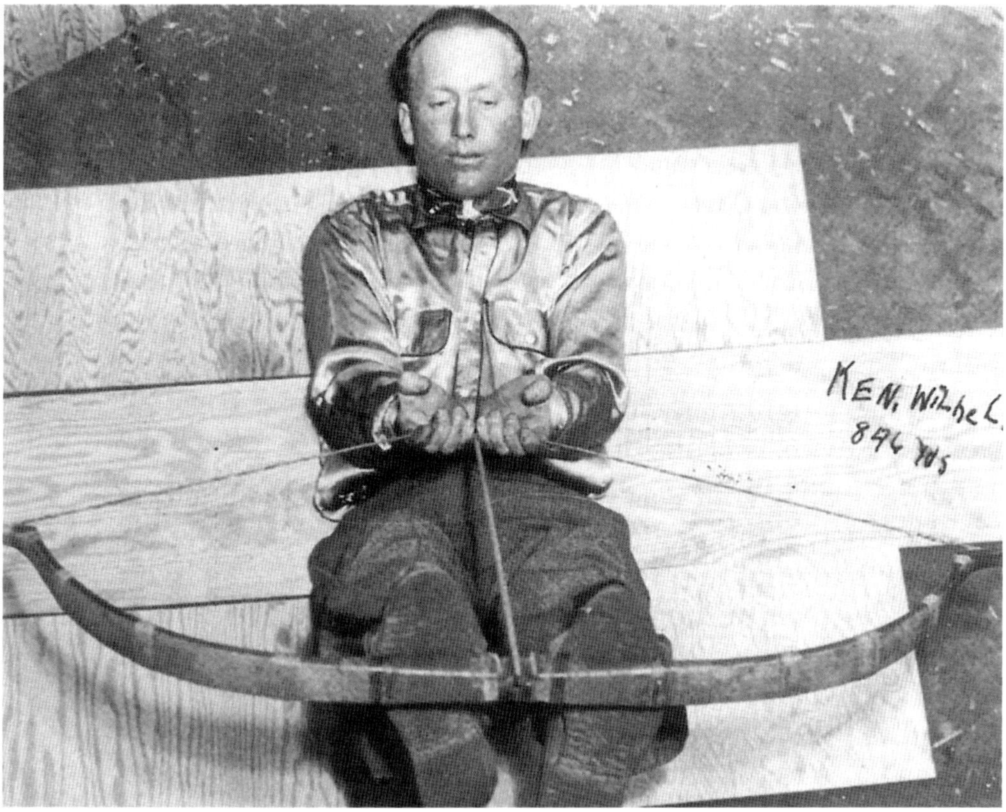

Image 29. Ken and his foot bow.

They appeared on lots of radio and TV shows and starred in four short films for Paramount: *Death Valley Thrills*, *Like Father, Like Son*, *A Desert Adventure*, and *Meet the Champs*. Until 1954, they performed in practically every North American, and even some European, live shows. Saying their tricks were outstanding would simply be an understatement. In 1938, in *A Desert Adventure*, Ken shot a biscuit out of Walt's mouth and a sugar cube off his ear. Walt had an unusual anchor point, drawing the string to his hip because he had repeatedly broken his shoulder when he was a young man. Both Wilhelms were so-called snap-shooters and Ken could shoot left-handed as well as right-handed. In one of his stunts, Ken shot a collar button and a dime off Walt's head from a range of 30 feet. At the same distance, Walt lit a match that Ken held between his fingers—another spectacular Whilhelm brothers stunt. They were said to be the first ones to use artificial smoke on their shafts to follow an arrow in flight. Even though their tricks were hair-raising, the Wilhelm brothers never had an accident.

In a short film starring Howard Hill, he first shoots an apple then a plum off a costumed fella's head using a broadhead arrow. When Hill places a cherry on his "assistant's" head, the costumed fella runs away as fast as he can. The assistant was Kenneth Wilhelm.

The Wilhelms didn't use their own homemade bows exclusively. Ken had a 70-pound yew flatbow with silk backing made by Fred Bear that he called Rib-Splitter and Walt had a short, broad 65-pound Osage bow from Ben Pearso n named Hells-Bells.

Ken traveled around a lot, organizing field ranges for various clubs in the US. Some of Walt's friends were authors—Captain Jack Willard, who wrote *The Cat and the Canary,* and Erle Stanley Gardner, author of the Perry Mason books. Walt, himself an author, wrote *Last Rig to Battle Mountain*, allegedly an autobiography about a miner's family moving through Nevada around the turn of the previous century. The book is regarded as a true account of the pioneer life

When reading old books about archers like Ken and Walt Wilhelm, the old times come alive. I get a bit nostalgic when I think of the spirit these men had. I believe the most important thing for them was not how well they shot or how much game they took; the most important thing for them was the fun and the comradeship.

References:
Howard Hill, *Hunting the Hard Way*
Craig Ekin, *Howard Hill: The Man and the Legend*
Fred Anderson, *The Traditional Way, The Mystique and Heritage of Archery*
J.E. Davis, *Ye Sylvan Archer* magazine

Image 30. Walt on his favorite horse, Old Chief.

Hugh Rich

Hugh Rich

Image 31. Hugh Rich, 1948.

From the 1920 to the 1950s, California was the center of archery in the US. Even though the number of archers and clubs was on the rise in other states, California, with its mild climate, offered year-round shooting and tournaments. The young Howard Hill left his home in Alabama to go to California, where he established an archery range and wrote the first rules for archery golf, a popular sport back then.

Lots of other famous archers like Saxton Pope, Art Young, Frank Eichholtz, Captain Jack Hoefer, Erwin "Doc" Pletcher, the Wilhelm brothers, Ed Hill, Captain Cassius Styles, Art Lambert, and James Duff, as well as numerous famous archery enthusiasts like Guy Madison, Roy Rogers, Errol Flynn, Gary Cooper, and Erle Stanley Gardner could be found in sunny California. A Californian one should know, is Mr. Hugh Rich.

Houston Duane Rich was born on November 16, 1916, in Glendale, California. At the early age of five, he went hunting with his father for the first time.

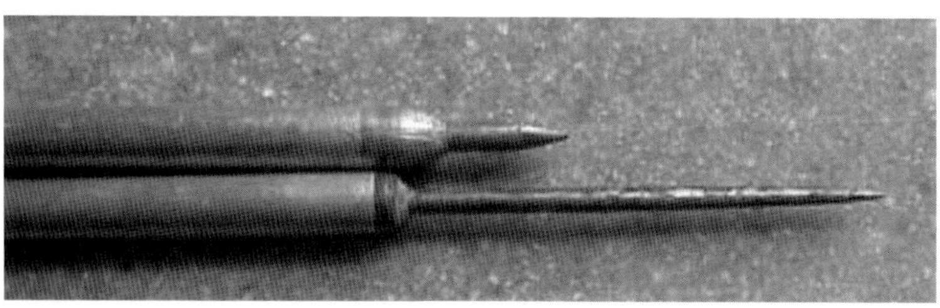

Image 32. Archery golf arrows.

Around 1926, Hugh Rich discovered the bow and arrow and spent much of his free time at the Griffith Park Archery Range. He retrieved arrows or wrote down the scores of champions like Saxton Pope, Art Young, and Captain Jack Hoefer. Captain Jack, as people used to call Hoefer, showed Hugh how to make arrows, a skill he learned well from Mr. Will Thompson, no less. Even at this young age, Hugh had a talent for fletching; using the pin method, he was able to fletch 60 shafts in an hour—that's one shaft per minute and 20 seconds per feather.

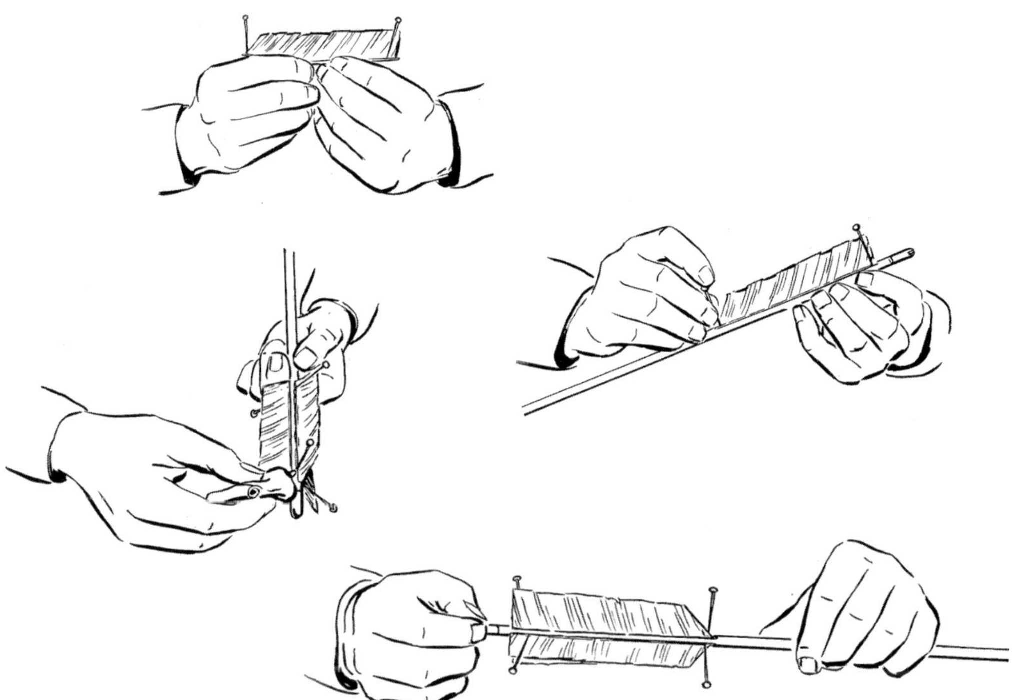

Image 33. The pin method.

I used to fletch my first arrows with the same method, but it took me a little longer—I could keep a pace of almost 60 minutes per arrow.

In those days, the quills were not split and ground like today, they were "stripped," that is, they split the center of the quill of a full length Turkey feather, then put it into warm water. Then they stripped off the feathers and the skin around the quill. Excess skin was cut off and the feathers were shortened to the necessary length.

For a long time pins were used for fletching. The feathers, shortened to a certain length, were held onto the shaft with pins. Then the quill was coated with glue on the left and right. After drying for 30 minutes, a second layer of glue was added to the quills. Then the arrows were allowed to dry for an hour. After that, the feathers were either trimmed with a pair of scissors, cut with a wooden or metal trace, or burnt off with a glow wire.

Captain Jack Hoefer, an accomplished archer and archery shop owner, was very impressed with Hugh Rich's abilities and his assiduity. He gave young Hugh a job in his archery shop. Many famous archery champs were among Captain Jack's satisfied customers.

In 1936, Hoefer wanted to retire and offered to sell his shop to Hugh. The Captain wanted \$200 dollars. Hugh did not have enough money and asked his father for a loan. Later on, Hugh found out that the shop was worth well over \$2,000. He suspected that his father had worked out some kind of secret deal, but he could never prove it.

Over the next years, Hugh Rich was able to expand to become a well-known outfitter of archery equipment. Among his customers were famous Hollywood stars like Gary Cooper, Bing Crosby, Roy Rogers, Guy Madison, and Iron Eyes Cody. Hugh Rich was acquainted with practically every famous bowman and a large number of people working in the film industry. He manufactured archery props for lots of films. It is likely that he made Errol Flynn's original quiver, which has since been lost, for *The Adventures of Robin Hood* in 1938. Similarly, Howard Hill provided bows and arrows and served as stunt archer for *Captain of Archers.* I think Hill worked together with Hugh Rich to source the archery supplies for this film.

Among Hugh's specialties were arrows with rubber or rubber foam broadheads, which he manufactured in great number for cowboy films.

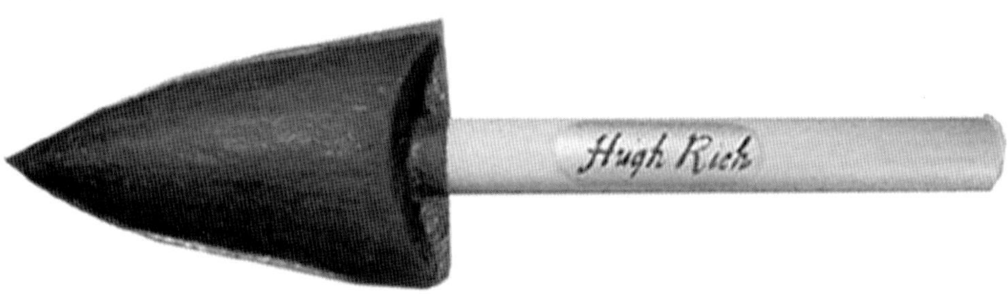

Image 34. Prop arrow with rubber arrow head.

After taking over the shop, one of Hugh's largest orders was 100 lemon wood longbows for the University of Southern California.

Over the years, Hugh made more than 6,000 bows. In addition to his many other qualities, he was exceptionally good at making arrows. When Howard Hill was preparing his safari to the Belgian Congo (c. 1950), he had Ben Pearson make ten gross of arrows (1,440). The arrows were then brought over to Hugh who was asked to check the spine, straightness, clean nock alignment, and fletching stability. Hugh worked them over when necessary and crest-coded them. I learned from a reliable source that after *Tembo*, the film about Hill's safari, was released, Hugh's relationship with Hill had soured. Perhaps Hugh Rich had expected to read his name in the opening or final film credits: "arrows by...," or something like that. But Hugh Rich was not mentioned at all, and the relationship remained strained for some time. Maybe Howard had made an exclusive deal with Ben Pearson, but I was not able to find that out.

More than 25 National Field Archery Association (NFAA) champions used Hugh Rich's arrows. Hugh himself was an excellent shooter and bowhunter. From 1947 to 1949 he was second in the NFAA bowhunter class. He won first place in 1950.

Fred Anderson, a friend of Hugh Rich's, wrote in his fantastic book, *The Traditional Way: The Mystique and Heritage of Archery,* that he had asked Rich who was the best field archery shooter in its heyday in California. They had a lengthy discussion about Larry Hughes, Ande Vail, Howard Hill, Ken Wilhelm, Roy Dill, Erwin Pletcher, and many other great archers. Rich finally came to the conclusion that Larry Hughes was the best. Then he changed his mind and said that Roy Dill, the 1948 NFAA champion, was the very best. In 1948, there were so many excellent field archers that only a champion could be the best of the best. Roy Dill and his brother Bob were trick shooters who performed in various shows in the 1950s.

In addition to his accomplishments on the archery field, Hugh Rich was influential in other ways. He served as president of the Southern California Field Archery Association from 1951 to 1957. During the 1950s, there were so-called anti-archery groups which wanted to forbid shooting the bow and arrow in Los Angeles County. I cannot understand why. Rich fought for the rights of the archers and won the first national trial against such a group.

Hugh Rich cofounded and became vice president of the Archery Manufacturers and Dealers Association (AMADA), an organization later known as AMO, that standardized bow and arrow measurements and names. Even today, most bow manufacturers still stick to the AMO names and standards.

Hugh Rich was also a founding member of the California Archery Hall of Fame in 1977.

Image 35. Perfect arrows.

The introduction of the compound bow had a lasting impact on the archery scene worldwide. This new device, which could be obtained everywhere, made hunting and shooting with relatively little training, talent, and power possible. The mighty dollar started to dominate archery, and this once marginal sport was gradually commercialized. Less time was needed for training and perfect materials were cheap and readily available. These developments may have had a gradual, disintegrating effect on the archery community. Doesn't that sound familiar...

Authors like Fred Anderson and Wade Phillips, who knew Hugh personally, wrote that he got melancholic when he remembered the golden times of archery from his youth. In those days there was a bond of friendship and sportsmanship amongst shooters. Slowly, the number of Hugh Rich's archery friends dwindled.

The revival of the longbow in the 1980s and the resulting resurgence of a traditional archery scene that relied on old values and bow types, delighted the 70-year-old Hugh Rich. In the last years of his life, Hugh Rich corresponded with old and young shooters alike.

Mr. Wade Phillips, historian and expert on broadheads, Bear equipment, and many other aspects of American archery, is the author of two meticulously researched works, *Broadheads 1871–1971: Identification and Rarity Guide* and *Traditional Broadheads 1972 -2002: Identification Guide.* Phillips sent me the following e-mail, after I had asked him for information on Mr. Rich:

Hello Peter,

Yes, Hugh Rich was a fine fletcher. Not many people alive today know that. In the 1920s he learned the art of arrow making form Capt Jack A Hoefer and then in the 1930s he bought Hoefer's archery business and continued a life long involvement in archery. In 1905 Will Thompson said that Hoefer was Thompson's most promising student. Hugh Rich was a good friend of mine for many years.

In 1982, I spent a week at Hugh's home in Burbank, California. His health was failing him and he had serious back problems. His garage was 2 cars wide and 2 cars deep and so full of old archery equipment, books and magazines, that stuff fell out the door when I opened it. Clearing a narrow path through the garage to be able to see the items was nearly impossible. Hugh bought out many old archery shops in California that had gone out of business over the years. Hugh saved all of the out of date equipment from these old shops. When Hugh's old friends passed away, he was the recipient of most of their archery memorabilia. Hugh had many rare items that I have never seen before. He was not a collector in the sense that we think of the organized collector today, but rather he was a saver of anything to do with archery. Hugh had more old original Howard Hill equipment than anyone I have ever met. He had all of John Yount's memorabilia, items from Walt and Ken Wilhelm, Roy Hoff, Nubbie Pate, you name the old time California bowman and Hugh had some of his stuff.

Hugh does not get enough credit today for his contributions to archery and his foresight to save so many items for us to enjoy as collectibles.

Good Hunting & Shooting
Wade

In 1990, the highly talented Hugh Rich died. I would love to have one of his perfect arrows on my wall.

References:
Fred Anderson, *The Traditional Way: The Mystique and Heritage of Traditional Archery*
Wade Phillips, e-mail correspondence
The Archers Hall of Fame website: www.archeryhalloffame.org

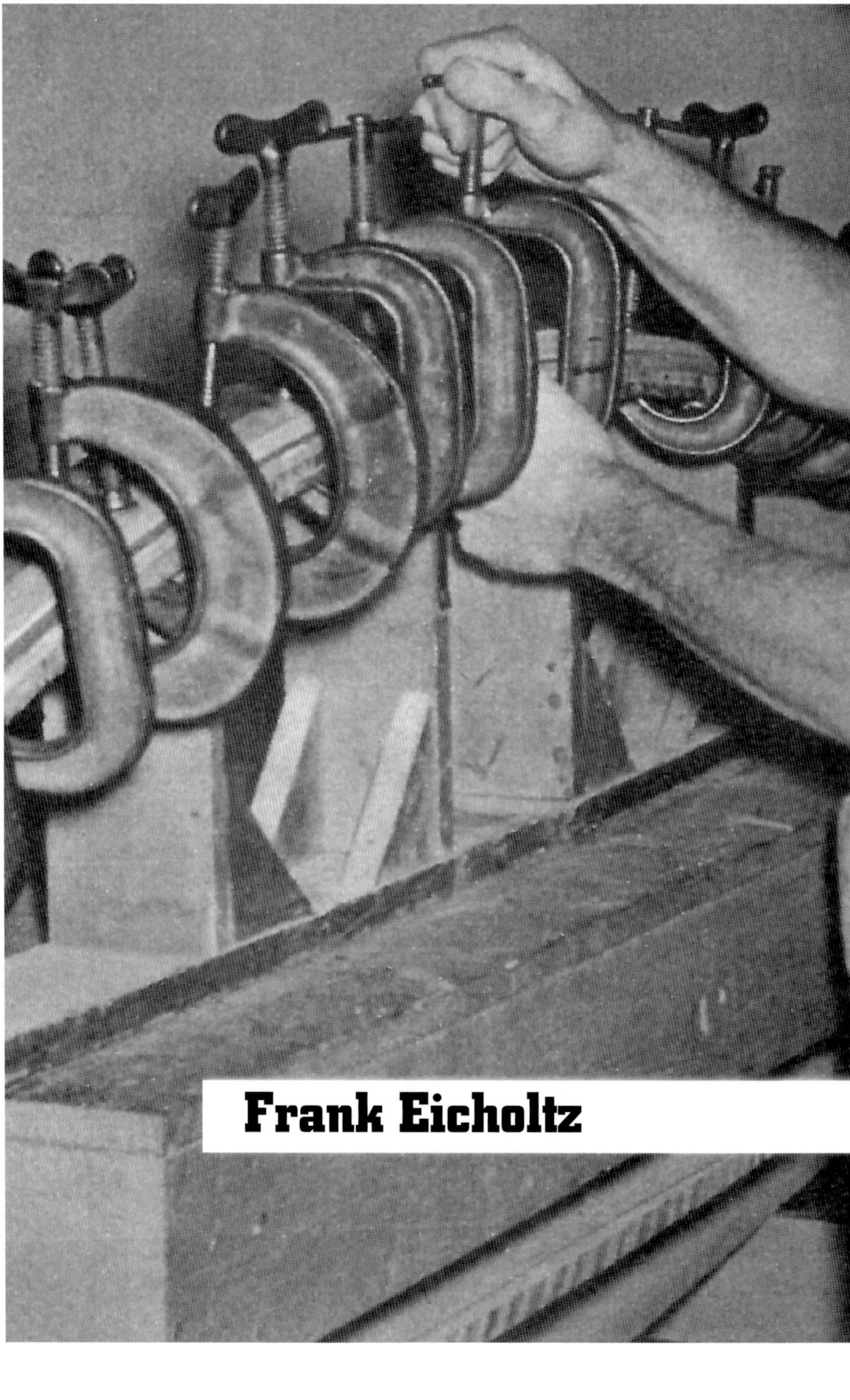

Frank Eicholtz

Frank Eicholtz

Image 36. Frank Eicholtz shooting.

Some technologies and materials, taken for granted by today's archers, are not that old yet. A good example is the use of fiberglass for making bows. Shooters and bowyers racked their brains over how to make bows, which often break easily, more durable. An efficient, high-end wooden bow is like a Formula 1 race car. And of course, its always the fast, slim, favored bows that break first. There is only a small number of materials that can prevent bow breakage caused by overstraining and temperature fluctuations. An "overbuilt" bow, with too much wood and some spare inches in draw length, won't shoot smoothly or fast, but handling it will be easier and it will usually be more durable.

Old tournament archers tried to have two or three identical bows (99% yew), to be able to participate until the end of the tournament with a similar "sisterbow" just in case of bow breakage. The bows were shot alternately to maintain, more or less, the same performance and characteristics.

It was a long journey from the Native American's sinew backing to rawhide backings to backings made from textiles like silk to pressed paper backings like Fortisan to today's bow technology, which utilizes glass fiber and carbon. Even though the materials have changed, the same method is used for fiberglass and the old, reliable sinew backing. It's a tried and tested technique that has been used for thousands of years to prevent breakage. Just like the sinew backing, fiberglass increases the draw weight of the bow. Other backings, like rawhide or textiles, only provide some kind of protection against mechanical wear and do not make the bow more efficient. They hardly increase the draw weight of a bow.

At first, only backings were applied, later on facings were also used, but not all fiberglasses were suitable for both backings and facings.

I have old Howard Hill bows from the 50s and 60s. These bamboo-lam bows were backed with woven "Pantherglass," tillered, and then faced with linear fiber glass. The various kinds of fiberglass had different characteristics. Some of them were more suitable for tensile load, others more suitable for compressive load. Today's glassed bows can remain braced without causing any damage—at least that's what some claim. I believe it is better to unstring them.

Frank Eicholtz from California is the innovative man responsible for our modern, very durable, and consistent bows that maintain their casting power. By the early 1940s, Frank had become very experienced in making bows, coming to the conclusion that the composite bow, as used by the Turks and Asian cultures, had its advantages over other bow types. He experimented with various materials, for example lamicoid, a plastic material used for making company signs. This material seemed to work well. World War II brought many new technologies and materials. Many things that we use every day have roots in military inventions—fiberglass is such a material.

Narmco, based in San Diego, California, is the world's leading company in fiberglass technology. They are responsible for woven fiberglass sheets called conolon. Fishing rods were also made from this new material. Eicholtz backed some of his bows with this new conolon fiberglass and used lamicoid as facing. Mr. Henry Drake, a well-known bowman in those days, used a 50-pound composite bow that was "tuned" by Eicholtz for flight shooting. The average flight shooting range, using normal bows with up to a 100-pound draw weight, was about 490 yards. Drake shot Eicholtz's 50-pounder over 600 yards, setting the archery world on fire.

Many, maybe most, of today's mass-manufactured traditional bows consist of two layers of glass fiber, with a core of various lams. Very often maple or mountain maple is used.

Mr. Eicholtz discovered this wood for his composite bows. He had mainly used yew, the classic bow wood, as a core. But yew would not tolerate the pressures and the heat when glassed. After numerous experiments, Frank decided to use maple as his core wood. Maple was cheap, available, mechanically durable, and it glued well. Frank began producing his modern bows commercially and archers were delighted by his bows, their consistent casting performance, and incredible effectiveness.

Howard Hill, back then the star of the archery scene and a clever bowyer himself, had re-discovered bamboo as bow wood. He heard of Eicholtz's revolutionary bow-making method and asked him to back and face a couple of his bows with fiberglass. Hill was thrilled by the result, a result he had been dreaming of for a long time—speed and consistent performance. Eicholtz taught him the new method and supplied him with bow material for many years.

In the 1950s, Eicholtz's bows and the "Eichholtz glass" were increasingly in demand throughout the US. George Gordon, a friend who was making fiberglass signs at the time, affiliated himself with Frank and they were soon selling fiberglass to bowyers around the world. Everything was fine until Frank contracted a terrible infection that had him on bed rest for several weeks. During these weeks Gordon sold, what Eicholtz believed, was a large amount of bad-quality fiberglass. Their sales stagnated until his business was ruined. Frank was bitter and never forgot this disaster for the rest of his life.

Soon afterwards Eicholtz got together with a man from Costa Mesa, California, and started his fiberglass business anew. He developed fiberglass arrow shafts, later known as Micro-flite arrows. But Frank barely turned a profit with this business as bad luck struck again. His partner died in a car crash, and the patents for his Micro-flite shaft were not properly secured. Frank lost another promising business.

Manufactured by a different company in the 1960s, Micro-flite arrows and shafts were sold worldwide in large numbers—you can imagine how angry Frank must have been. I have some of these Micro-flite arrows. They are light brown, spine-coded, and tapered towards the nock. Bob Swinehart and Bill Negley used these durable shafts on their safaris.

The Bowlock was another unique invention by Frank Eicholtz. It was a simple release aid. Today we know all the mechanical release aids that compound shooters use: plier-like devices or release mechanisms that use a rope and attempt to guarantee a clean release despite acute bowstring angle. Frank's release was a non-mechanical one. The bowlock was hooked over the bowstring released by the thumb.

Therefore it was a very popular and legal release aid in NFAA tournaments.

During the 1970s, many shooters and bowhunters decided to use the new and more effective compound. Traditional bowyers had to give up their shops and wooden arrows were replaced by aluminum, fiber glass, and carbon arrows. It wasn't until the late 1980s that archers worldwide rediscovered the longbow and the recurve. It was during this decade that the term "traditional" was defined, distinguishing it from compound archery and other high-tech archery gear.

Frank Eicholtz was an inventive traditionalist. In answer to the compound, he built very fast recurves using the most modern laminates. He used, for cxample, graphite and boron. The limbs had extra long recurve to compete with the compounds back then. I contacted some owners of these Eicholtz bows and they all assured me of their excellent quality.

Frank Eicholtz died in 1983. This man had a lasting influence on our modern bow technology. He was the first bowyer to use plastics, a maple bow core, and fiberglass as backing and facing. He was the first to develop functional fiberglass arrows and invented the first Center-Shot Takedown bow handle and an efficient bowstring release aid.

And still, most archers today have not heard much of him.

I believe Frank Eicholtz's most revolutionary invention for archery and the traditional bow was his use of fiberglass. Nobody I know has been able to convince me of the advantages of carbon, a trendy material used to make bows today, nor have I seen proof that it increases performance.

If you hold a fiberglass laminated recurve or longbow in your hands, you should think of the truly ingenious inventor of these good bows.

References:
Fred Anderson, *The Traditional Way: The Mystique and Heritage of Archery*
Keith C. Schuyler, *Archery: From Golds to Bit Game*

Ben Pearson

Ben Pearson

"*Big, fat 'gator-garfish', Ben.*" Hearing these words on the phone, which raised the fine hairs on his neck, Ben looked towards his desk next to the wall. There was a prototype of the new takedown model. The bow was completely coated in fiberglass and had a maple core. Its ergonomically designed leather handle hid a takedown system. This "molded" design with the wooden core and the fiberglass was absolutely new; even today, I still don't understand it completely. How was the maple core (solid or lams) completely molded in fiberglass? I have such a bow, it is 64" long and is marked 50#@28". Over shorter distances, it casts passably, but not very fast despite its narrow bow tips. However, it is quite a nice, functional, beautifully designed bow. My bow looks as if it were made of caramel-colored horn. If you take it apart, you can easily transport it in the quiver. Sometimes I use this old timer for bowfishing. I love using old bows, often discovering that they are able to compete with many modern bows.

Howard Hill had promised Ben to advertise the new bow. The brochures had already been printed. They also wanted to make a short movie. Ben Pearson, Howard Hill, Ken Jones, Red McGovern, and Tom McGhee would meet at the White River in Arkansas to hunt the big garfish with the bow. These primeval animals can weigh up to 300 pounds and their heads look like alligator heads—even the teeth look similar.

Howard explained the following to Ben on the phone, "Eh, Ben, let's gotta go out there and knock out some of these big fellas—with ya new glassy toy bows."

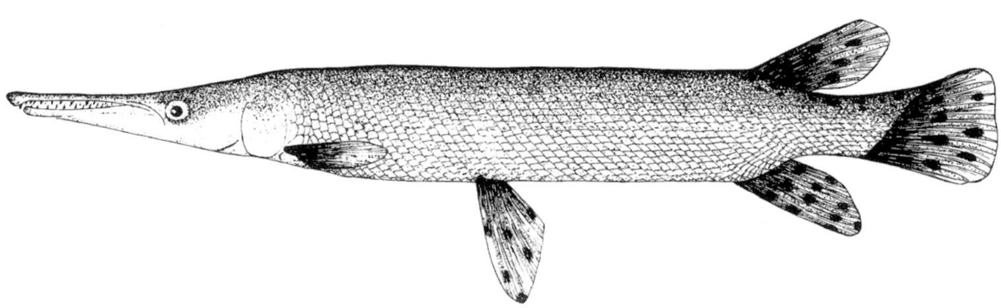

Image 37. Alligator Gar, Lepisotsteus Spatula.

Ben could hear how much Howard was looking forward to their trip.

"We'll arra 'em, from boats an' than we'll catch out these beasts with a big fish rod, uhh we're goin' to have real fun there at the river, don't we?"

"Just manage the film crew, Ben, an' we'll do just what we like to do, the movie guys should film us at—so we 'll get no pressure to do any actin' or so".

Ben immediately liked the idea. Combining fun and work was exactly what he wanted. Mr. Hill was not only an excellent archer, he was also a mastermind when it came to marketing and organizing ideas and get-togethers of that kind. Ben Pearson immediately agreed with him. He knew the thing would work and it would be fun, there was no need for any special arrangements or a screenplay. Ben would only have to contact a film crew and to provide the equipment. All bowmen would be provided with the #304 fiber glass "Takedown," the official name of the bow. And of course, he also provided for a sufficient amount of fiber glass arrows with fish heads.

Image 38. Ben Pearson

Ben Pearson was born on November 16, 1898, in Saline County, Arkansas. Dan Beard, a Boy Scout troop leader, sparked Ben's interest in archery. Ben made his first bow following Beard's instructions. It was a typical English longbow made from hickory with horn nocks, just like bows were made back then.

Well, either Mr. Beard had not counseled young Ben much or maybe he did not want to re-do it, but Ben finished the bow with a draw weight of 90 pounds. However, Ben was able to bag some birds and other small game with it. Soon afterwards, Ben heard from another bowyer—Mr. William S. Morgan of Little Rock, Arkansas. Young Ben spent some time with Morgan and learned a lot about bowmaking and the various materials. Ben quickly acquired some useful archery tackle. In 1926, Ben took part in the Arkansas State Archery Championships in Little Rock. He placed next to last of 20 shooters. This poor showing did not discourage him, and he upgraded his equipment and improved his shooting technique. The next year he placed first in Little Rock and Ben was Arkansas State Champion. He was on the right path. Over the next ten years Ben was a regular competitor at tournaments.

In 1926, Ben started working for the Arkansas Power & Light Company as an electrification specialist. As you can imagine, the electrification of rural areas was a profitable business in those days. He remained with that company for five years. In his free time he was selling arrows that he made in his garage. He was known for his "footed arrows," made from cedar with a four-splice hard wood footing.

As the Great Depression deepened, the Arkansas Power & Light Company stopped its electrification project in the backcountry. They respected Ben's hard work and offered him another position within the company. Ben turned down their offer because he wanted to dedicate himself to his true passion, developing and producing archery equipment—not at all an easy venture. But fate would play in Ben Pearson's favor.

Mr. Carl Haun, a retired oil man from Blackwell, Oklahoma, who had invested his money buying oil, mining, and newspaper shares, purchased a bow and arrow set for his grandson at Christmas. Typically, it didn't take the grandson long to lose or break all his arrows. Well, why should we care about that? The grandson wanted to have more arrows and Gran'pa Haun set about contacting various arrow makers. When Carl Haun heard about Ben Person's archery shop in Arkansas, he got onto his private plane and went to Little Rock. Ben told the very interested Carl Haun about his dream—mass production of bow equipment. In 1938, Mr. Haun returned to Little Rock and asked Ben to find "For Sale" signs on buildings. Ben came upon an old, shut down mill with a "For Sale" sign on it. Carl Haun's financial backing, Ben Pearson's mechanical knowledge, and a 7,000 square meter factory all came together as the Ben Pearson Company.

In his younger years, Ben Pearson was one of the most successful target archers. In 1938, he was seventh behind Pat Chambers in the National Archery Association Annual Tournament, twenty-four places ahead of another young talent—Fred Bear, a bowmen from Michigan.

Ben Pearson and Pat Chambers, a top-notch shooter, became friends and Pat would soon promote Ben's archery tackle. Later, Ben Pearson held shooting performances for young people, especially Boy Scout troops.

In the 1950s and 1960s, Ben performed live in lots of TV shows, including the popular Will Rogers Show. Quite contrary to many of his colleagues, he never charged anything when performing. He only wanted to promote archery and do what he enjoyed most—shoot the bow and arrow. Ben showed an impressive number of tricks in his short films. Standing on a quickly moving boat, Ben shot at balloons floating in the water. From the same rocking boat he shot at clay pigeons and through rings tossed into the air. One of his best known tricks was to shoot through the hole of a vinyl record in mid-air.

When Ben Pearson began bowhunting in Arkansas there was only little game. However, in 1955, he was able to take a stout whitetail, the first one to be officially arrowed in Arkansas. Ben loved bowhunting, especially small game. But he also took delight in bowfishing the alligator garfish. He was taken with these fish, which were more than two meters long and could weigh up to 300 pounds.

Image 39. Ben Pearson and his hunting companions.

Image 40. Ben Pearson's Skeleton Broadhead.

In the beginning, leather products like quivers, shooting gloves, tabs, etc., where bought from Fred Bear's Bear Products Inc. Ben produced high-quality bows made from yew, Osage, lemonwood, and hickory. His arrows were well-known for their good quality, especially the hollow cedar arrows he developed for tournament shooters. In 1943, the Ben Pearson Company started its own leather production. In 1938, Ben Pearson developed his first broadhead, a "Skeleton-Broadhead" made from steel. Most of us know this design, the Australian "Ribtek" hunting heads by Col Graham are similar.

Ben developed a special forked broadhead for hunting birds. The forking should prevent the arrow from bouncing off the game. Ben made a short movie about a pheasant hunt where he used a forage dog, bow, and arrow. The film depicts many incredible shots at flying pheasants.

In 1948, the company name was changed from Ben Pearson Company to Ben Pearson Inc.

According to some authors, Ben was the global leader in supplying archery tackle in 1950. Three hundred employees produced several hundred high-quality, low-priced bows and more than 12,000 arrows a day. I don't know if Bear Archery or Pearson had the higher output or who was the first to mass-produce bows.

In the 1950s, the fiberglass takedown, described earlier in this chapter, was introduced. It was available as model #306, 66" with a draw weight of up to 85 pounds; model #304, 64"; and model #302 with 60". The bow was intended to be low-priced and suitable for everyone in America—ladies, youngsters, and children. Legendary bowmen Howard Hill advertised this fine bow for Ben.

Image 41. Deadhead and Switchblade.

The most striking Pearson hunting head was probably the Deadhead, developed for hunting turkeys. The Deadhead was extremely broad and vented, which was very effective when hunting tough turkeys. In 1964, this broadhead was offered under the name #777 or Deadhead and it soon became one of the most popular hunting heads. Consequently it was used for hunting any kind of game. There were two designs available: a 1 5/8" broad, 175 grains version and a 1 3/8" broad and 130 grains version. Bob Swinehart, for example, took some of his African trophies with a Deadhead.

In 1974, Ben changed the name of the company again to Pearson Archery and he produced another broadhead, the Switchblade. It was 130 grains and had a replaceable bleeder blade, similar to Fred Bear's Razorhead. The additional, replaceable blades resulted in a four-blade hunting head. Like Bear's Razorhead, the bleeder blades were made from flexible spring steel. The two advantages were that they broke off or apart easily and the head was sharper.

In 1987, the Silver Tip, Pearson's first screw-in head, with 90, 100, and 110 grains, was introduced. This broadhead came out as a three- or four-blade model. Presumably, Ben Pearson also developed the first handy, portable taper tool. So, for

Image 42. Bill Negley testing arrows with Ben Pearson.

the first time archers were able to taper their shafts everywhere, not just at home, but out in the woods and in meadows.

In 1956, the Bushmaster bow, which would become Ben's hallmark, was released in 60" or 64" lengths with laminated maple fiberglass limbs. At first, the bow was offered in the catalog, rather unimaginatively, as a "Laminated Takedown Recurve." However, archers called it Bushmaster, and starting in 1958 it was found under this name in the Pearson catalogue. As the hallmark bow, Pearson continually improved and offered Bushmaster in various lengths, draw weights, and center shot-designs.

Image 43. Pearson Takedown system.

Even though, years ago, I tidied up my bow nook and gave away all my recurves to make room for some longbows and my old Bear Cub and a Bear Custom Kodiak Takedown, I'd love to have a Bushmaster. I used to have an interesting old Pearson bow, an Ambusher, a tiny recurve that was only 48". My first longbow was a Ben Pearson Ol' Ben—a 68" longbow that was not very fast. It had 50#@28" and it was a rather boring bow with broad shovels. There was not a Ben Pearson feel to it.

Between 1956 and 1959 Ben Pearson made various hunting films. Ben and his companions took javelina, pronghorn, mountain lion, wild goose, and pheasant with Pearson tackle. There are many extraordinary shots in these movies. For example, Dr. James L. Smith, a hunter and friend of Ben's, killed a javelina from about 70 yards with an incredible shot. Accompanied by the Bushmaster and Deadheads, Pearson flew to Alaska in 1965, killing the most powerful grizzlies and polar bears taken with a bow and arrow up to that point.

In 1962, Ben Pearson Inc. had more than 500 full-time employees. Every day the facility produced 36,000 arrows and 3,000 bows. From 1960 to 1965, in addition to the Pearson standard product-line, the company made Locksley products, low-priced tackle for archery novices. From 1961 to 1968, the Golden Sovereign line was released featuring superb, high-end bows.

With his enthusiasm, technical know-how, willpower, and various other admirable qualities Ben Pearson, just like Fred Bear, was an archery pioneer, leaving an everlasting footprint. He developed machines for manufacturing bows and arrows, providing high-quality and affordable archery tackle within the means of every archer.

In 1967, the industrious Ben Pearson retired. He passed away on March 2, 1971, at age 72. After his death the company was sold several times and all the machines and production lines that Ben had developed disappeared. Today, Pearson Archery leads a shadowy existence compared to the erstwhile popularity of Pearson tackle. In his forty active years, Ben Pearson created millions of archers. Bows and tackle from Ben's golden era still electrify collectors around the world.

In 1972, Ben Pearson received his well-deserved place in the Archery Hall of Fame, and in 1996, the National Sporting Goods Hall of Fame.

Image 44. Howard Hill, Ben Pearson, Bo Graf, and Ed Hill near the Colorado River.

References:
T.J. Conrads, *The Traditional Bowhunter's Handbook*
Craig Ekin, *Howard Hill: The Man and the Legend*
Rick Hinton, *Instinctive Archer Magazine*

Sasha Siemel

Sasha Siemel

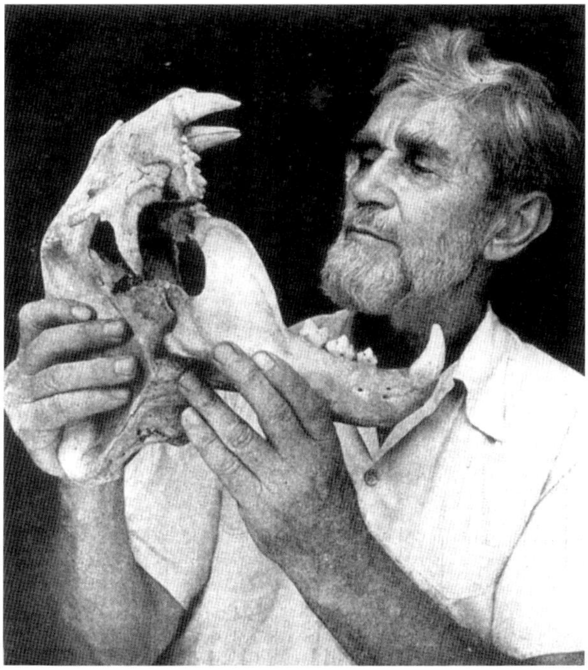

Image 45. Sasha Siemel

Ever since I was a child I have liked true adventure stories, accounts by and about explorers, captains, airmen, trappers, detectives, mercenaries, toreros, and hunters. These included the books and experiences of T. E. Lawrence, Lawrence of Arabia; Henry Morton Stanley, famous for his search and rescue of Dr. Livingstone; Gerhard Rohlfs' travel accounts; and General von Lettow-Vorbeck's books about the war in Eastern Africa. And it didn't end there. I always thought Ladislaus de Almásys, who became famous as The English Patient, was a real Indiana Jones. Almásys found the mythical oasis Zerzura in the Sahara desert with the help of an antique Greek book. And then there was Jim Sutherland's stories on hunting elephants and I devoured books by J. A. Hunter, Ernst Alexander Zwilling, and Peter H. Capstick.

Even though I'm in danger of being identified as the good-old-times and manly-adventure oddball, I do admit that I love these stories and books. Aren't we like soft, lazy mollusks compared to these oldtimers? I really don't understand the importance of today's idols, I don't give a dam about David Beckham whose latest hair style is, of course, less interesting to me than, for example, the broadhead that Art Young used. Maybe I have a hopeless case of macho ignorance.

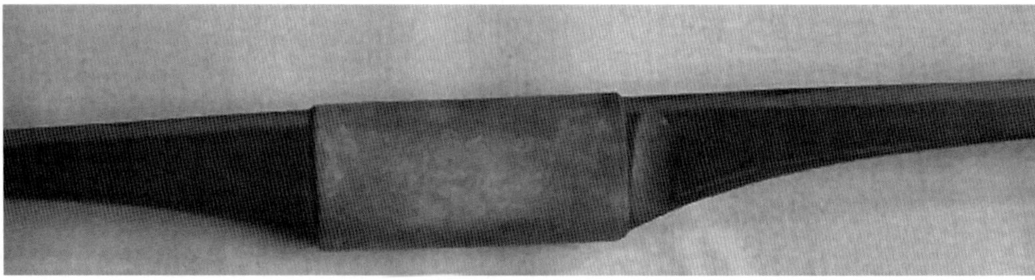

Image 46. Sasha's bow, owned by Ted Fry. The scuff marks show that Siemel was a real archer.

Well, I don't have anything against these modern "heroes," but what I admire about the old ones is that apart from being adventurers, apart from their outdoor qualities, they were able to read and write.

Alexander "Sasha" Siemel isn't "the" archer par excellence. He used a simpler weapon, but he also hunted with the bow and arrow and was acquainted with Art Young, enough for me to "impose" him on you.

In 1937, Sasha Siemel wrote, "When I was very young, I felt the stirrings of wanderlust and an overpowering desire to live an adventurous life. I determined to do everything I could do to live life to the full—to taste the exotic sweetness of freedom."

Doesn't that very poetically put message reflect the spirit of a truly adventurous hero?

I bought Sasha Siemel's book *Tigrero!* for a few dollars in an American antiquarian bookshop. I knew his name and was looking forward to reading about hunting adventures in the Brazilian rainforest. It exceeded all my expectations; in other words, I was thrilled by this prototype of an adventurer. I believe Siemel is one of the most interesting characters of the last century. He was an explorer, guide, prospector, lecturer, soldier, photographer, author, boxer, hunter, mechanic, and gunsmith. He spoke six languages and even lectured in Europe. Unfortunately, I could not find out anything about these lectures. Howard Hill was also in Europe, but I only came across a photograph taken at the World Expo in Brussels.

Those who have heard of Sasha Siemel know that he hunted Brazilian jaguars or *tigres*, powerful, big cats weighing as much as 400 pounds. Sasha killed 30 of them armed with a homemade spear, the Zagaya. Very often, ranchers needed Sasha's help to dispatch dangerous jaguars that were terrorizing and killing their cattle. Over the years, the Tiger-man killed 270 jaguars with rifle, bayonet, spear, and bow. (Protection of species or animal welfare did not matter in those days.)

Image 47. El Tigre, taken with a spear.

The bow and arrow were Siemel's usual tools of trade. He did not use the bows of the Native Brazilians but longbows of American origin. In 1937, in a letter published in *Ye Sylvan Archer*, Sasha mentions a bow that he received from Bob Faas, a well-known American master.

We all know that real archers have always had, and will always have, a particular interest in adventures. It is quite easy to understand how Dr. Robert Elmer, a well-known archer and author, became acquainted with the Tiger-man who was on a lecture tour in the US. Elmer introduced Sasha to American archery and taught him proper, modern shooting techniques. He also put Siemel in touch with Art Young. Due to their love of adventure, the two would develop a friendship lasting until Art Young's early death. From the 1930s to the 1950s, Sasha became well acquainted with the American archers, shooting with Erle Stanley Gardner, George Brommers, and the Wilhelm brothers. He was a member of the "Lower Bracket Boys." Sasha never missed a chance to needle his fellow archers. Upon learning that Gardner had missed a moose Siemel said, "He is a wonderful marksman as long as he isn't shooting at anything."

Alexander Siemel was born in Latvia in 1890. At the age of 16 he had to choose between living with a rich aunt or beating it. He decided to get away from home and boarded a ship in a search to find his older brother Ernst. In 1907, Sasha arrived in North America. At first he wanted to go to New York, but went to Chicago by train instead. He was learning English while working as a waiter, liftboy, and factory worker. He also held positions in a candy store and boutique.

Image 48. Zagaya

Then, working as cook on board a ship, Sasha went to Buenos Aires, Argentina, where he learned Spanish. While in Argentina he started working in a print shop. He developed a friendship with a German who was living with his wife in Buenos Aires. A dramatic love story sprang up between him and his new friend's wife—it was one of those stories where nobody is to blame but everybody suffers. After talking things out, Siemel ended the relationship with a heavy heart. He was tormented by his ambivalent feelings, having betrayed the German who had been a good friend to him on the one hand, but on the other hand, he felt sure that he was leaving the love of his life for good. Sasha Siemel, always the restless one, quit the field, hoping he had not completely ruined the couple's marriage and that the two German's would become happy again. He spent three years in Buenos Aires, the longest he would ever stay in one town. Sasha was corresponding with his brother who served in the Argentinean Army, but was smitten with Brazil. In *Tiger Man,* Julian Dunguid quotes one of Ernst's letters to Sasha about Brazil: "Every forest trail, is a finger pointing to Eldorado."

Siemel wanted to go to Brazil, a mysterious and wild country in those days. He had heard about diamonds and the Matto Grosso, a vast wilderness. He wanted to look for those diamonds with Ernst in this endless grassland, with ample stock of game, and where cattle rangers were leading a rough life.

Sasha found Ernst Siemel in Passo Fundo, a small town in the south of Brazil. They were making plans for their future, while working as mechanics and locksmiths to earn a living.

Image 49. Frank Buck (left) and Sasha Siemel (right) in *Jungle Terror.*

There are many stories from their stay in Passo Fundo worth mentioning, for example, boxing matches between Sasha Siemel and professional wrestlers. With the money he won in the match, Sasha bought a donkey and named it Beduino after his defeated opponent.

Dom Carlos, the unofficial sheriff of Passo Fundo, was a friend of Siemel's. They often enjoyed lengthy conversations about the country and its people. Dom Carlos told him about an old Indian hunting the *tigres* with a spear and some dogs. That piqued Siemel's interest and he tried to find out everything he could about this Indian and his whereabouts. However, their conversations weren't always fun. Sasha complained he was being provoked by a man named Ricardo Favelle. The sheriff warned him not to offend or attack this man in public, as he would not shy from killing a sleeping man. But Favelle humiliated Siemel at every possible opportunity. Dom Carlos advised Sasha either to avoid any conflict with Favelle or to kill him, but if Sasha killed his enemy, he, Dom Carlos, would be after Sasha. To put some emphasis on his words, Dom Carlos asked Siemel to have a look at a string over his door. There were dried human ears on it, in various states of preservation. Nice times for outlaws, don't you think?

However, one day, there was a fight when Favelle ambushed Siemel and tried to kill him with his pistol. During their hand-to-hand fight, Sasha hit Favelle with the pistol on the head and Favelle collapsed. Sasha was shocked and fled, he was sure he had killed his attacker. Later on, he found out that Favelle had only been unconscious. Out of friendship, Dom Carlos gave Siemel a head start, knowing what a filthy rat Favelle had been. Then he carried out his duty picking up Sasha's trail, but he was not rushing, not following as quickly as he had followed the owners of those dried ears.

Sasha met his brother Ernst at a certain meeting point they had previously agreed on. They moved from ranch to ranch, repairing all kinds of machines: sewing machines, pumps, rifles, pistols, etc. Sasha always asked the gauchos and ranchers for the Indian hunting the *tigre* with the spear. One day, they found this man, who really did exist. His name was Joaquim Guato and they found him drunk, surrounded by his pack of dogs in a humble hut. They agreed to meet the following day to hunt together. Sasha brought his Winchester and his photo equipment with him, Joaquim his dogs and the Zagaya, a homemade spontoon-like spear with a cross guard at the end of the blade, which prevented the speared *tigre* from attacking the hunter over the spear shaft. The blade was fixed onto a strong wooden shaft and the whole thing had a length of about six and a half feet. It sounds quite sporty to me.

Usually, the dogs hunted the jaguar into a tree, where they trapped it, barking at the cat long enough to annoy it and make it attack the man with the spear from the tree. An important fact to be mentioned: one should never ever let go of the spear. That sounds logical and simple enough—if a big cat of about 400 pounds attacks, you really need to sweat it out with your six and a half foot spear until the *tigre* is dead. Maybe even more interesting was how Joaquim faced the jaguar, attacking fast as lightening on the ground in order to fight it. I think it is impossible to imagine that kind of fight—their courage makes Joaquim Guato and Sasha Siemel some kind of modern dragon slayer. Guato and Siemel usually hunted and fought alone, accompanied only by their dogs. There was usually nobody who could have helped them if anything went wrong.

In 1923, Sasha found employment as a professional hunter, dispatching jaguars for ranchers. At first he armed himself with a rifle. In1925, he killed his first *tigre* armed with only a spear.

In 1929, the author Julian Dunguid went to Brazil where he met Sasha Siemel. They embarked on a trip across the Pantanal, a vast tropical wetland. In 1931, Dunguid gave

Sasha the name Tiger-man in his novel *Green Hell.* Later the same year, with the help of Dunguid, Siemel received an invitation to lecture about the Pantanal and his hunting adventures in England for the members of the Explorers' Club. In 1932, Julian Dunguid published Siemel's biography *Tiger Man.*

Image 50. Julian Dunguid, Mamerto Urriolagoitia, J.C. Bee-Mason, and Sasha Siemel.

In 1937, while lecturing at the University Club of Philadephia, Sasha met the 18-year-old Edith Bray. She was so impressed by Siemel that she convinced her parents to allow her to join Sasha in his Matto Grosso expedition. Miss Helen Post, an acquaintance of Siemel's (by the way, when did he have time for women?) who had wanted to go to Brazil for a long time, accompanied them as their chaperone. Edith Bray, even though she had some initial qualms and disapproved of hunting, turned out to be an enthusiastic hunter. Once when Siemel was fighting a jaguar something went wrong and he managed to shoot himself in the leg with his .44 revolver. If that doesn't mean a thing to you, a .44 is quite a weapon. I assume that the bullet did not penetrate the bone, otherwise the leg would have had to be amputated. It took the two young ladies and some of Sasha's native helpers two weeks by packhorse and oxcart to bring the wounded Siemel into a hospital.

Edith made another trip to the Matto Grosso as a photographer. In 1938, Sasha appeared in the 15-episode serial *Jungle Menace* as Tiger Van Dorn. It was a real cliffhanger. I have the DVDs, which are very cool. From time to time you can see Siemel armed with a spear, uttering a few pithy, heavily accented words. In 1946, the serial was compiled into a film, released under the title *Jungle Terror.*

In 1940, Edith and Sasha were married. Edith had obviously convinced Sasha that her being 28 years his junior didn't matter to her. What is it that women like about these machos?

Sasha's wedding present for Edith was a 50-pound yew longbow made for her by Dr. Klopsteg.

The Siemels lived in the beautiful Pantanal in Brazil, on their houseboat called *Aventureira.*

There are various books about the Tiger Man: *Green Hell* (1931) and *Tiger Man* (1932) by Julian Dunguid, who embarked on the Green Hell trip with Sasha as his guide.

Jungle Wife (1949) was written by Sasha and Edith Siemel and Gordon Schendel. *Tigrero!* (1953), *Jungle Fury* (1954), and *Sashino: The Story of Jaguar Hunt in Brazil* (1965) were all penned by Sasha. In 1952, he wrote the article *The Jungle was My Home* for the National Geographic.

Tigrero! was to be made into a movie starring John Wayne and Ava Gardner, but 20th Century Fox Studios never shot it. According to the *New York Times* it would have been too expensive to insure the stars while filming in the jungle. In 1996, *Tigrero: The Film That Was Never Made*, a documentary by the Finnish director Mika Kaurismäki was released. In 1981, Peter Hathaway Capstick describes Sasha Siemel's adventures in *Death in the Silent Places.* I believe that Capstick's biographies of legendary hunters are perfect examples of informative, non-fiction adventures.

Alexander "Sasha" Siemel, the Tiger Man, died in 1970, in Green Lane, Pennsylvania.

I am afraid that the cloth from which men like Sasha Siemel are cut is becoming scarce. Luckily, there are at least books that make it possible to follow the trails of these adventurers.

Fortunately I was in contact with Alexandra Sondra Siemel, Sasha's daughter, in 2009. She's still living in Pennsylvania. Every year she travels back to Brazil to stay for some weeks in the places of her childhood, where her Dad, the *Tigereo,* hunted and lived. Sondra was very helpful and she was happy to hear that Sasha Siemel is not forgotten and still has many fans around the world.

Image 51. The versatile Tiger Man, back when men were still drinking whisky.

References:

Sasha Siemel, *Tigrero!*

Julian Dunguid, *Tiger Man*

Julian Dunguid, *Gree Hell*

Gene Wensel, *The Best of Traditional Bowhunters*

Fred Bear

Fred Bear

Image 52. Fred Bear

We all know this gentleman. He is a lean, tall man in a Borsalino Hat with a weather-beaten face, a red-checkered shirt, camouflaged jacket, and a recurve bow and quiver under his arm. He is looking out into the vast, open land.

When I took up archery, Fred Bear was more or the less the only well-known archer in Europe. That is because every archery shop, mainly hunting outfitters in those days, only sold Bear archery tackle. And they had Bear catalogues, which I got my hands on whenever possible. Of course, I didn't give a dam about the compound bows in the catalog, I preferred looking at the photos of Mr. Bear. He was usually accompanied by really nice fellas like Canadian moose, Alaskan grizzlies, and Indian tigers. And sometimes with really nice fellas like Apollo astronaut Jim Lovell and actors like William Shatner. That was Fred Bear.

It would take me a few years until I had read about his life and his adventures. Until then, he was like some mythical creature for me—the biggest bowyer of his day, hunting in Africa, India, South America—a real outdoorsman and a cool guy who knew how to turn his passion into a successful profession.

Various books about Fred Bear have been published in the meantime. It is impossible to cover all the adventures this most impressive man had in just one chapter. I will try to give a chronological overview presenting the most important facts about the man with the Borsalino Hat. People who knew him personally and every publication about him always described Papa Bear as an extremely innovative, determined, but also very modest and nature-loving man.

Image 53. Leonard Osberg, Art Young, Carl Strang, Fred Bear, and Ray Stannard.

1902

Frederick Bernard Bear was born on March 5, near Waynesboro, Pennsylvania. His parents, Harry Leon Bear and Florence Bear, née Drawbaugh, had Bear in their farm house during a terrible blizzard. He had an older sister, Ailenn, and later a younger sister, Elizabeth.

1915

Harry Bear takes 13-year-old Fred on his first hunt. They are hunting whitetail, in an area known as South Mountain Ridge about five miles from the farm. Even though he was still a boy, Fred started setting up traps. With the money he received for the fur he trapped he purchased a motorbike for $35.

1916

Fred takes his first whitetail, a buck, with a rifle.

1918

The Bears move to Carlisle, Pennsylvania, where Fred attended high school.

1919

Fred Bear serves with the Carlisle National Guard Cavalry.

Image 54. Fred Bear, on the right.

1920

Fred is employed by the Carlisle Frog & Switch Company as a pattern maker. I suppose, today, we would call that a die maker.

1923

A few days after his 21st birthday, Fred Bear boards a train to Detroit, Michigan, where he begins work as a die maker for the Packard Motor Car Company. In the evenings he attends the Detroit Institute of Technology. He lives in a small room on Lothrop Avenue.

1926

Fred becomes plant manager of the Jansen Manufacturing Company, which makes spare tire covers for automobiles. In those days, the spare tires of most automobiles were trunk-mounted on the exterior of the vehicle.

Image 55. Blaney Park, Michigan.

Image 56. Bear in 1927.

1927

Fred sees Art Young's film, *Alaskan Adventures,* at the Adams Theater in Detroit. He later meets bowhunter Art Young at a Rotary luncheon and the two became friends. They build archery tackle in Fred's basement and begin shooting together.

1929

Fred goes bowhunting for the first time in a swamp near St. Helens, Michigan.

1930

Enthusiasm for the bow and arrow becomes popular throughout the US. Indoor archery facilities and field ranges are widespread.

1931
The International Archery Federation (FITA) is established.

1933
In a small building in Detroit, Fred Bear and Charles Piper found the Bear Products Company. They mainly produced silk-screened advertising materials. But off in a corner of the building, Fred makes archery equipment. It soon becomes a full-time business for him. Due to the booming archery scene, there is an increasing demand for leather products such as quivers, arm guards, and shooting gloves. Only a minor part of the operation is dedicated to making bows—their primary business is making leather equipment. Fred Bear helps form the Detroit Archery Club.

1934
Fred wins the Michigan State Target Championships.

1935
At Blaney Park, in Michigan's Upper Peninsula, Fred shoots his first whitetail with a bow and arrow.
Bear Products Company, now known as Bear Archery, moves to a bigger location at Burlingname and Broad Street in Detroit.

1936
Two Michigan counties introduce the first bow season.

Image 57. Whitetail, 1935.

1937

First statewide bowhunting season in Michigan. Fred Bear files a patent application for his modern shooting glove. He wins the Michigan Field Archery Championship.

1939

Fred Bear wins the Michigan Indoor Spring Tournament. He moves his company to a third location in Detroit. The National Field Archery Association is established.

1942

Jack Van Coevering, sports editor of the *Detroit Free Press*, produces the first bowhunting film with Fred Bear at Blaney Park, a large hunting area in Michigan's Upper Peninsula.

1943

Fred begins work on his first takedown bow. He wants to make a functional, simple system, easier to travel with in bush planes.

1945

Near the north end of Lake Wabaskang, at the mouth of the Cedar River in Ontario, Canada, Fred takes a moose with a bow, his second big game trophy.

Image 58. Moose, 1945.

1946

At the age of 68, Fred's father, Harry, won the National Archery Association (NAA) Mail Matches. Fred makes his second bowhunting film, *Moose Diary.*

Fred Bear takes his first black bear with bow and arrow near the previous year's camp at Lake Wabaskang.

Bear Archery patents the use of fiberglass as bow backing. In a bold move, and perhaps unlike what many others in his place would have done, Fred allows the entire archery production industry to use this breakthrough technique for free—for the good of archery worldwide. In 1946, Fred Bear secures the first bow quiver patents. The bow quiver, just like the Borsalino Hat, becomes another Fred Bear trademark. Reading Dick Lattimers book, *I remember Papa Bear*, you will realize that Fred was an excellent marketing strategist. He chose a certain outfit to make people remember and recognize him. A part of Fred Bear, as we know him from his photographs, is an artificial character. Mr. Bear knew how to cooperate with the media and how to promote his adventurous hunting stories and inventions. Bear often used his bear trophy, a standing Alaskan bear he had killed in 1960, during promotional tours and exhibitions. He associated the trophy with his company's emblem, his own name, and Bear products.

Fred knew that if hunting with the bow became an independent sport and form of hunting in America, it would also become a huge market for Bear Archery products.

1947

The new Bear Archery plant opens in Grayling, Michigan.

1949

Fred develops a new bow bonding process. It is the first year that Bear bows get registration numbers and warranties. The Grizzly bow is introduced.

1951

Fred develops a special press for bow bonding and patents are granted for his unidirectional glass fiber used as bow backing and facing. Fred begins bow hunting in the Western US.

1952

Fred harvests his first elk and first pronghorn antelope in Wyoming. Fire nearly destroys the plant in Grayling.

Image 59. Bear with bear.

1953
The plant is rebuilt.

1954
Bear produces the first working recurve bows (Kodiak II). Fred bags a mule deer.

1955
Fred becomes a member of the Adventurer's Club. The Bear Archery plant in Grayling reaches 100 employees. Fred goes hunting overseas in French Equatorial Africa. In Canada he kills moose and caribou.

1956
Bear Archery plant is enlarged and expands to 200 employees. Fred markets the Bear Razorhead.

1957
In British Columbia Fred takes a world record stone sheep.

Image 60. Nelson Grumley, master bowyer. His bows are very sought after today.

1958

Fred hosts the 13th National Field Archery Association's (NFAA) National Championships. The first Pope & Young Club awards are held in Grayling, Michigan. Fred hunts the Little Delta in Alaska.

1959

The Fred Bear film library comprises thirteen productions. Fred again hunts the Little Delta in Alaska.

1960

Fred develops and patents clear Crystalight Bearglas. He hosts the NFAA National Championships with twenty-six field ranges in Grayling. He takes a world record Alaskan brown bear.

1961

Bear Archery introduces the Fox line of solid fiberglass bows, affordable bows for children and youngsters. The Professional Archers Association is founded.

1962

Fred appears on *To Tell The Truth*, a national TV program.

1963
Bear Archery markets snap-on bow quivers. *Life* magazine features Fred's grizzly hunt in British Columbia. Invited by the Maharajah of Bundi, Fred hunts Bengal tiger in India.

1964
Fred Bear starts the advertising campaign, "Become a Two-Season Hunter," enticing rifle hunters to enjoy an additional hunting season with Bear bow and arrow products. Fred is awarded the Compton Medal of Honor. He hunts big game in Africa, taking an elephant with a bow.

1965
Fred embarks on his third African safari in Mozambique accompanied by professional hunters Wally Johnson and Bob Munger. Bear takes a lion and cape buffalo.
(I recommend Bob Monger's book, *Trailing a Bear,* to everyone interested in Fred Bear's adventures. He describes some of their hunting trips in an amusing way.)
Bear Archery starts the production of high compression handle material. Fred appears TV again, this time on the show *American Sportsman.*

1966
Fred appears on the *Tonight Show* and is inducted into the Sporting Goods Hall of Fame.
Fred Bear takes a polar bear on the third try.

1967
The Fred Bear Museum opens in Grayling, Michigan. Fred Bear perfects his takedown system. Bear Archery is sold to Victor Comptometer Corp., but Fred remains president and begins selling his products worldwide.
The 48" Super Magnum recurve is introduced. Fred takes an Asiatic buffalo on Marajo Island, Brazil.

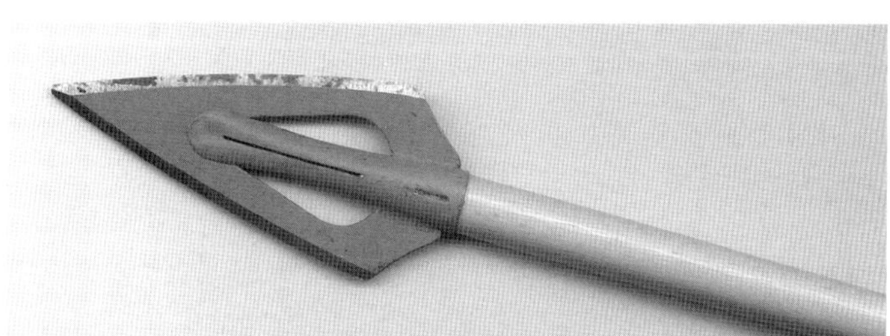
61. Bear Razorhead.

1968

Bear Archery produces Converta-Point arrows. A recording of an interview with Fred Bear and Curt Gowdy, *Secrets of Hunting*, sells 60,000 copies. Fred receives the Michigan Governor's Award and Doubleday Press publishes his first book, *The Archer's Bible.*

1969

Fred Bear appears on *The Mike Douglas Show* with Gentle Ben. The first US World Championship Target Tournament is held in Valley Forge, Pennsylvania.

1970

After extensive field tests, Fred Bear's Takedown bow is introduced. The new Futurewood handle material is also marketed. During the Bear American Archery Tournament, the Fred Bear Sports Club is established by Dick Lattimer at Detroit's Cobo Hall. Champion archers, astronauts, and TV stars are among its first members, including William Shatner. The Bear Archery film library now comprises twenty films.

Image 62. Fred, the tiger, and the Maharajah of Bundi, 1977.

Image 63. Fred and Wally Johnson in Mozambique.

1971
Fred introduces magnesium alloy handles for his Takedown.

1972
Archery becomes an Olympic sport.

The Astronauts Charles Duke Jr., John Young, and Thomas Mattingly take one of Bear's Razorheads on their Apollo 16 voyage to the moon. The Archers Hall of Fame is established and Fred Bear is among the first to be inducted. The Fred Bear Sports Club publishes a *Code of Outdoor Ethics*. Every sportsman may now join the club, which launches its own magazine, *The Big Sky*.

1973
Fred is inducted into the Hunting Hall of Fame.

1976
A labor strike against Bear Archery is organized by the United Auto Workers Union. However, many employees continue their work and some replacement workers are hired to keep production going and meet customer's demands. The Bear plant produces a record 360,000 bows in one year. Fred's second book, *Fred Bear's Field Notes*, is published by Doubleday Press. Fred receives the Lifetime Career Award from the National Sporting Goods Association. Winchester/Western's Outdoorsman of the Year award is given to Fred Bear, and the University of Michigan grants Fred the Regent's Citation.

Image 64. Asiatic buffalo, weighing nearly one ton.

1977

Apollo 8 and 13 astronaut Jim Lovell and Fred film *The Good Earth*. The Fred Bear Sports Club helps launch *The American Outdoors* TV project. Fred receives the NAA's Maurice Thompson Medal of Honor.

Walter Kidde & Co. takes over Victor Comptometer Corporation and Bear Archery.

The Maharajah of Bundi and his wife are guests in Fred's house in Grayling, Michigan. Fred visited the Maharajah in India in 1963 while on a tiger hunt.

1978

Bear Archery markets the Bear Super Razorhead and the plant is moved to Gainesville, Florida.

1979

Fred's third book, *Fred Bear's World of Archery*, is published by Doubleday Press. Fred also engages in the construction of fiberglass automotive springs.

Image 65. Quality check.

Image 66. Carp fishing.

1980

Fred is featured on Glen Lau's *Sports Afield* television series. The Fred Bear Signature bow is introduced.

1981

A second plant is opened in Williston, Florida. It produces fiberglass springs for cars and other non-archery products. The Fred Bear Sports Club now has 50,000 members from the US and 44 countries. Bear Archery introduces the stainless steel Razorhead and the Delta-V bow, the world's fastest bow. Fred is admitted to the North Florida Sports Hall of Fame. Fred becomes member and guest speaker at New York's prestigious Boone & Crockett Club, founded by President Theodore Roosevelt in 1887.

1982

Fred's 80th birthday is celebrated with surprise visits by guests from around the country. Fred gets the Sporting Goods Manufacturers Association's Extra Mile Award.

1983

Bear Archery celebrates its 50th Anniversary.

1987

Fred is honored by the Safari Club International Hunting Hall of Fame and the SCI Bowhunting Division Hall of Fame. Fred receives the Conservation Career Achievement Award, given by the National Wildlife Federation and the Minnesota Conservation Federation.

Image 67. Fly-fishing in Grayling, Michigan.

1988
Fred Bear dies on April 27 from a heart attack at the University of Florida's Shands Hospital in Gainesville, Florida. His cremated remains are placed along the Au Sable River near Grayling, Michigan, not far from a small chapel, where he used to fly-fish. The location is accessible only by riverboat. Fly-fishing was, right after archery, Fred Bear's second greatest passion.

I have always regarded Mr. Bear as the personification of the American dream, he was a self-made man, who really did it, who made his way with ambition, great ideas, and determination. He always remained honest and stuck to his principals, whether he was hunting or doing business.

The following quote from his *Field Notes* is characteristic for Mr. Bear:

> *A downed animal is most certainly the object of a hunting trip, but it becomes anticlimax when compared to the many other pleasures of the hunt.*

References:

Fred Bear, *Fred Bear's Field Notes*
Charlie Kroll, *Fred Bear, Biography of an Outdoorsman*
Bob Munger, *Trailing a Bear*
Fred Bear, *The Archer's Bible*
T.J. Condrads, *The Traditional Bowhunter's Handbook*
Dick Lattimer, *I Remember Papa Bear*
Time line: www.bowhunting.net

Ande Vail

Ande Vail

Howard Hill was the most famous Hollywood trick shooter. But there were others, too. One of the best was Ande Vail, who was born in 1920 in California. At the age of ten he started shooting a bow and by the time he was sixteen, he was making money with archery. He attended high school with Hugh Rich.

Around 1938, Ande opened an archery shop, a real store with plate glass window. It was at this time that Ande started doing trick shooting. In 1942, he became known as "Mr. Trick Shot." He performed more than 8,000 times for the US Army. Among his tricks were "framing" somebody with his arrows, shooting them around a volunteer, or the popular shooting an apple off somebody's head or a cigarette out of somebody's mouth. These tricks are not recommended for imitation.

Image 68. Trick shooting, a very popular attraction.

Ande Vail also worked for major Hollywood film studios doing countless stunt-shots in Cowboy and Indian films. Ande did twenty-one short films, some of them on bow hunting. Unfortunately, I haven't seen them and I have found very little about Mr. Vail searching the Internet.

Image 69. One of Ande Vail's tie-on broadheads (c. 1940).

Ande Vail died in 1985 in Boise, Idaho.

Hugh Rich said of Ande Vail:

> *I have known about every great archer in the last 50 years—Erwin Pletcher, Roy Dill, Erwin Ketzler, Frank Eicholtz, Willard Bacon, Larry Hughs, Poky Quail, Howard Hill, Rause Hinman, Bob Poppe, Dick Tone, Russ Reynolds, and many more fine gentlemen who would have considered it a privilege to have traded shots with Ande on a one-to-one basis.*

And Fred Anderson said in his book, *The Traditional Way: The Mystique and Heritage of Archery*, that other famous archers would make sure that Ande Vail did not compete at the same archery tourney—otherwise, to come in first would have been impossible.

References:

Fred Anderson, *The Traditional Way: The Mystique and Heritage of Archery*
Rik Hinton e-mail correspondence

Howard Hill

Howard Hill

Image 70. Howard Hill, 1933.

San Diego, California, USO Event, 1948—An athletic man, wearing white polo shirt and white trousers, enters the stage. The hall is full. There is a back quiver full of arrows on his right shoulder and a slim longbow in his left hand.

"This is Gran'pa, my 85-pound split-bamboo-longbow, my baby. Let's see, what this bow is capable of", says the archer who has the looks and moves of a movie star.

The man takes an arrow out of his quiver and shoots it right into the tiny, black cross in the middle of the target butt, right into the bull's eye. The arrow disappears completely, as it penetrates the butt, hitting the wall behind it.

The archer smiles, looking unbelievingly-surprised at the bow, turns to the audience and says, "Well, I see, there is no arrow matching Gran'pa here. Looks like I have to shoot my 65-pound Gran'ma. Sorry, Grand'pa! The GIs are laughing.

The man takes another arrow, standing about 15 meters from the target. With unbelievable speed and precision, white-fletched arrows hit the bull's eye of the target. Within 26 seconds, Howard Hill shoots 12 arrows; the arrows are grouped so narrowly that he splits the nocks of two of them. The last arrow touches the red rings. Hill faces the audience and says, "Oh, I forgot to figure on the wind you made with your applause, fellas!" The GIs are laughing out loud. Hill turns towards the target again, shoots, kneeling, an arrow into the bull's eye, lies down onto a little bench, shoots, lying on his stomach and on his back, right into the middle of the target. Then he shoots, standing on one leg, holding the bow with the left shoe, drawing with his right hand, again splitting one of the nocks. Hill has an assistant, throwing wooden plates into the air, each of the blunt arrows hits home, breaking the plates. Then a short board, some kind of small ramp, is put down onto the floor of the stage. Howard shoots at the sloping board, the arrow ricocheting and hitting a balloon.

Howard Hill turns back to the marines, asking for a volunteer. A young GI goes onto the stage. Hill asks the soldier for his name, where his base was, and does a bit of small talk with him.

Suddenly, Hill asks the marine, "You're no one to become frightened, are you?"

"No, Sir"; replies the soldier. Howard takes the man to the target, saying to the audience;

"We'll see what this boy's made of."

Hill takes an apple out of a box, placing it gently onto the soldier's head, before he moves 18 or 20 steps backwards again. He looks into the eyes of the volunteer, warning him: "Now don't move a muscle." The marine is standing at attention. Howard raises his bow, nailing the arrow right through the middle of the apple.

Image 71. Doing trick shots from every possible position

Hill turns to the audience and says approvingly, "Not bad!"—"That's my favorite method to produce apple juice," he adds with a twinkle in his eye.

Then he takes a slightly bigger plum out of the box and puts it onto the head of the soldier who is looking quizzically at Hill. Howard goes back, saying again, "Don't move a muscle!" raises his bow and shoots through the middle of the fruit. Turned to the audience, Howard says, "Not bad!"

When Hill takes a cranberry out of the box, puts it onto the volunteer's head, confidently walks the usual distance back and turns towards the marine again, he only catches a glimpse of the soldier removing the fruit from his head, throwing it onto the floor, jumping off the stage as fast as possible. At that, Howard Hill says, smiling understandingly, to his audience, "Not too dumb, either!" The entire audience breaks into a rapturous applause.

In the 1940s, Howard Hill received $2,000 for a 30-minute-performance. A fortune, even by today's standards, if you think about how much he earned per minute.

At Grant Park in Chicago, Hill performed in front of 35,000 spectators. After the archery shooting exhibition, the crowd tore the shirt off his back and also took his bow and arrows for souvenirs.

Hill's characteristic shooting style has influenced generations of archers. He made reasonable, serious people who regarded the bow and arrow as kids' stuff, buy a longbow, don a back quiver, and shoot at really, really big animals. It was Howard Hill who made the longbow popular worldwide as a serious hunting weapon. Pope, Young, or Bear were not showmen of Hill's caliber—he really knew how to present himself and make the most of his shows. I think Howard Hill was the only one who made a living exclusively from archery.

Hill epitomized the perfect sportsman, typical for his era. He was an adventurer, able to enthrall others, a gentleman, and a tough guy at the same time. One might meet Howard Hill at a Hollywood party surrounded by movie stars fascinated by his Alabama-slang-Hill-stories—maybe when he was catching a bear in Wyoming with the lasso, or killing a dangerous shark, such a devious beast, with a longbow under water, using his homemade diving equipment, with Errol Flynn at the pump. One could also find Hill on Catalina Island preparing "Hill stew" at the campfire for his hunting chums after a bloodcurdling wild boar hunt. Once, to play a joke on his fellas, he also cooked a fox that he had bagged earlier. A typical Howard Hill joke.

Even today, lots of archers worldwide use the straight-ended longbow. Custom bowyers and major manufacturers, Martin Archery, for example, have this bow type in their program. Whereas, the simultaneous development of the modern longbow was moving more and more into the direction of "hybrid bow"—a heavy bow with a long middle section, often with recurve handle, and strong reflex-deflex limbs that shot arrows that were light as possible. Today's Hill-stye bows (with fiberglass) go back to the 1950s.

What is it that makes Hill-style bows so attractive? Purely rational and objective arguments will not give a watertight explanation why these simple, straight, plain bows with the deep, usually straight handle, still represent the upper limits of bow making for countless Hill disciples. What is it that makes these archers smile at modern longbow material?

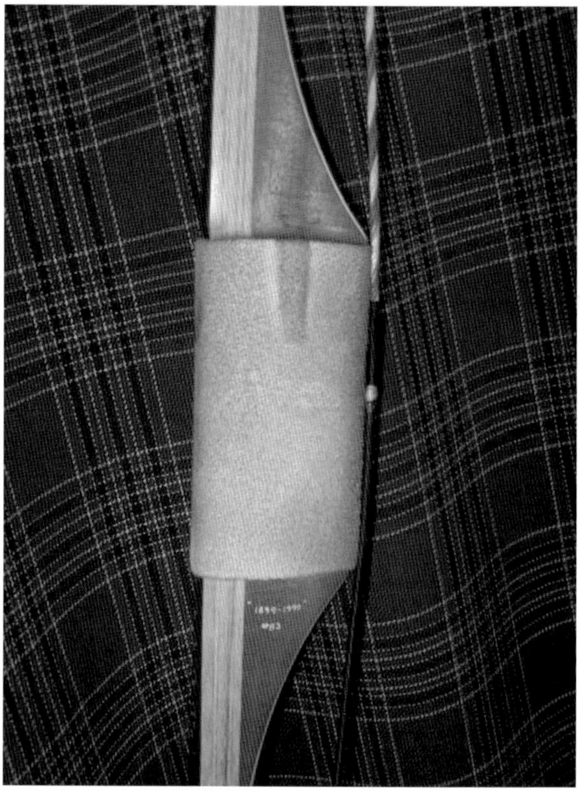

Image 72. Howard Hill Centennial, by Craig Ekin—simple and reliable.

I believe that it is Howard Hill's magic that works on these archers when they pick up their "bows of gnosis" and don their "holy" back quiver. A Hill-archer takes life easy, he knows that he surpasses all those losers on the field range, and it doesn't matter at all that he only ranks in the middle. However, what does matter is taking the right path, making the right choices, and maintaining tradition—that's it. Discussing who is shooting the heaviest arrow with a like-minded fellow is better. On Judgment Day, Howard Hill, dressed in white, will be sitting at the door to the happy hunting grounds of traditional archery, deciding on what is traditional and what is not. Better be prepared for it. That's something that the Hybrid-oddballs do not know.

It's a fact that there are excellent archers shooting Hill-style bows, also in Austria. But what is a Hill-style or Hill-bow?

Howard Hill himself called them "American semi-long bow" or "straight ended long bow." One can also regard these bows as direct descendents of the English longbow from the Middle Ages. During the 1920s, a type of bow modeled after the flat bow of the Native Americans and the classical English longbow, with a D-diameter, was built using yew, Osage, lemonwood, or hickory. Often, an additional piece of wood was glued onto to the bow as handle. You can see these bows in some early photos of Hill. Some mysteries surround these seemingly simple Hill-bows.

Image 73. Theo Schett, "Old Surehand," of Salzburg, Austria, with an 85-pound Howard Hill Big Five bow in South Africa, 2005.

John D. Lee knew Howard Hill; he was a friend and built the last three bows for Howard: Libba, Little Gator, and Slim Girl II. John described another one of Hill's bows to me in an e-mail: 63 pounds, 71", with a ¾ inch backset. Hill had shown John how to make a special concave-convex design. John D. Lee wrote the following when I asked him for his opinion of Hill:

> *Howard was a Man's Man as we say. Everybody liked him, he was able to develop his professional archery career because he met the right folks at the right time—like Glenn Curtiss. Howard's wife Elizabeth was ten years older, was a school teacher and loved him so he never had to go out and get a steady job after he married "Libba" as he called her. I met them both in 1973 at their retirement in Vincent, Alabama. Howard was a true archer, more than just a bowhunter, he loved the bow above anything else. He would be saddened about the way archery, even traditional archery has gone Hi-tech. He would not like deflex-reflex bows called longbows when they are nothing more than stretched out recurves...*

Well, that's the best way to put it, isn't it?

Image 74. When it came to equipment, Howard was a perfectionist.

Even though lots of archery pioneers and contemporaries of Howard Hill shot or made similar bows, the name Hill-bow became popular and widespread, probably because Howard Hill used this type of bow until his death in 1975. He said that recurve bows were too delicate for effectively shooting them. A controversial opinion, of course, until today. Nevertheless, Howard Hill Archery introduced recurve bows in 1959.

It is definitely justifiable to say that Howard Hill is the most famous archer worldwide—a fact that might have contributed to the rather general name "Hill-bow."

Hill's followers, like Bob Swinehart, John Schulz, Craig Ekin, Byron Ferguson, John D. Lee, and Bob Wesley, strict advocates of Hill's shooting style and Hill-style bows, encouraged the survival of this bow type, helping to make a legend. The shooting style and the bow type are as effective and functional as sixty years ago. Just watch a video or DVD with Bob Wesley or Byron Ferguson shooting the bow.

I cannot say when exactly bows were first made from laminates, as we know them today. Principally, English longbows, made of two or three laminates, have been made for a very long time (probably since the 14th century).

William Thompson let us know his experiences with the bows of his time, describing the bows he shot in great detail:

> *I [Will H. Thompson, F&S, 1979] have used in the last four years in my own practice the following bows: Five self-lance; three backed-lance; three rosewood (backed); six beefwood (backed); four snakewood (backed); two self-snake (grooved back); four self-lemon (citronella); one backed wood, unknown to me made by Highfield, London; two self-Spanish yew; one lance and hickory and one self-lance, made by Aldred, London; Spanish self-snake, made by E.& W. Madle, London; Spanish self-yew; four snake (and lemon-back); two beefwood (lemon-back); two rosewood (lemon-back); one amaranth (lemon-back); two lance and*

Image 75. Hill-style

hickory and one self-lance, made by Horseman, New York; one rosewood (swamp ashback), made by King, of Kokoma, Ind.; four Bois d'Arc (hickory-back); one self-Bois d'Arc (Osage-orange); *one lance and hickory and one three-piece (hickory, cocoanut, and hickory), made by Rechard of Crawfordsville, Ind.; and one split bamboo, made by Conroy, Bissett & Malleson, New York. Also arrows by each of the above makers. Also by Walter Granger of Buffalo, N. Y., and by one or two other Americans and several English makers. Several of these makers have kindly sent me for examination, test, and approval or disapproval, samples of their goods, and I have tried to give my true ideas of the goods regardless of the result. Now, nearly all the goods had some defects. It seems scarcely possible to get a bow with no defect in it. Yet while the English bows were the most accurately constructed, the American bows proved by far the most enduring. The principal defect in the American bows lies in the lack of sufficient wood in the centre, causing the bow to bend in the handle and thus jar greatly, and both tire the arm and destroy the accuracy of the shooting. The split bamboo did not have this fault, but it bent most in the lower limb, the exact reverse of what it should. It has been put through the utmost strain a bow could have, and stood it perfectly, and has at last partially yielded only to neglect in allowing it to stand against a damp wall all night, whereby the glue in the lower limb became softened. A friend from Marietta, Ohio, writes me that his experience with the split bamboo was disastrous; but I can only say from my own experience that, barring the faulty bend, my bamboo was a magnificent bow.*"

This informative report brings us to Howard Hill's split bamboo bows. Even though he was still shooting the English longbow (without additional handle), Howard Hill began, around 1925, to add his typical handles. The result was a Quasi self-bow with additional handle. The bows were often backed with clarified calfskin and had no arrow rest. In Craig Ekin's book, *Howard Hill: The Man and the Legend*, there is an illustration of a split bamboo bow that Hill built for Frank Garske in 1939. This bow looks very similar to today's Hill-style bows. In 1940, the typical, deep, narrow, almost acute handle, typical for Hill's bows, was introduced. Hill used to coat his bows with "Black Fiber," pressed paper. Another "pre-glass" bow backing material was Fortisan. This fiber, produced for parachutes by The Celanese Corp., replaced silk, which had been hard to come by since Pearl Harbor. Dr. C. N. Hickman found out that Fortisan was a better bow backing than the previously used silk.

Howard Hill soon recognized the advantages that split bamboo had as bow material. The laminates consist of countless, unbroken bamboo fibers which considerably reduced the risk of bow breakage. Bamboo is light and sturdy, making it possible to construct narrow bows, at the same time enhancing their velocity.

During the 1950s, Frank Eicholtz started experimenting with fiberglass backings. This material, which had initially been developed for military purposes, was known as Conolon. Eicholtz used Lamicoid plastic as facing material. A typical flight shot in those years, with a bow of up to 100 pounds, was 490 yards. Harry Drake shot one of the new composite bows, a 50-pound flight bow, over a distance of 600 yards. Archery and bow making were revolutionized. Howard Hill always strove to improve his equipment. He had Frank Eicholtz glass his favorite bows, White Eagle, Gran'ma, and Gran'pa. Hill was impressed by their enhanced performance. After Frank had taught him the method, Hill began using fiberglass for all the bows he made. Later on he showed the art of Hill-bow making to the Schulz brothers, John and Dan.

After 1950, Howard Hill seldom made bows, only making one for a friend from time to time.

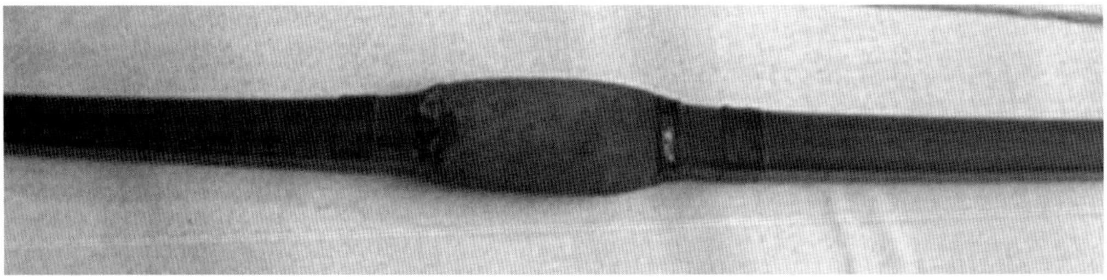

Image 76. One of Hill's typical English Longbows, owned by Ted Fry, Oregon.

There is one major difference between a Hill-bow and a modern longbow. The limbs of a real Hill-bow are high profile, they have a wider diameter—a Hill-bow is no flatbow. Therefore, I believe that it is more similar to the English longbow and more suitable for throwing heavier arrows than a flatbow. I am not a physicist, but I believe that due to the shorter handle zone and the steeper fade-outs, the working limb of the Hill-bow is longer than the ones of hybrid bows, which always have lengthened handle zones. There are some types of bows in between that look like pure Hill-bows, for example, a Martin ML-10 or ML-14. The handle section and the fade-outs are short, but their limbs are definitely flatbow-style.

I have seen a Jeff Challacombe red elm, Hill-style bow with fiberglass backing and facing (65# @26" 66") throw 580-grain arrows with 5 1/2" fletching at a speed of more than 200 fps. Karl Hofmeister was shooting them through a chronograph. These Jeff Challacombe (Queensland, Australia) longbows are the fastest Hill-bows I have ever shot.

As far as I know, from 1941 to 1961, Ben Pearson had the right to produce archery equipment under the name Howard Hill.

Image 77. Jeff Challacombe, Queensland, Australia.

From 1955 on, Ted Ekin, who, with Dick Garver, was running Shawnee Archery in Sunland, California, was a friend of Howard's. From 1958 on, Shawnee Archery produced and sold bow, arrows, quivers, etc. under the name Howard Hill Productions. In 1960, Howard Hill Archery Inc. was established and the company relocated to Sun Valley, California. Ted Ekin left Shawnee Archery in 1968, remaining the only one with the right to use Howard Hill's name for his products. He moved to Hamilton, Montana, and died in 1979. The family-owned company, headed by Ted's son Craig Ekin, still exists today. It makes high-quality Hill-tackle and bows with typical Hill styling, which it sells all over the world. Until 1981, when Craig began manufacturing Howard Hill-bows, renowned bowyers, like John Schulz, Ted and Lee Kramer, Tim Meigs, Jim Darling, and Dale Philips made bows for Howard Hill Archery. Lots of other bowyers offer Hill-style bows. Some of them decided to stick to this tradition after attending bow making seminars by John Schulz.

I have bows made by Craig Ekin, John Schulz, Pete George, Nate Steen, Jeff Challacombe, Dale Philips, and one, I believe, made by Jim Darling. All are real Hill-style and hard hitting, sweet shooting longbows.

In 1965, Howard Hill moved back to Alabama, where he was born in Shelby, on November, 13, 1899. His wife, Elizabeth Hodges Hill, a true Southern lady, wanted to go back home. Hill continued his cooperation with Ted Ekin. As long as Howard and Elizabeth were living, they received the profits made from archery equipment sold under Howard's name.

Image 78. Elizabeth Hodges Hill, or "Libba," as Howard used to call her.

From time to time I make and sell Hill-style quivers, even today profiting from Howard Hill's popularity—just like lots of other archery shops, bowyers, or archery clubs worldwide.

Howard Hill's books, *Hunting the Hard Way* (1953, Wilcox & Follet), and *Wild Adventures* (1954, The Stackpole Company), are real classics in archery literature.

Craig Ekin, author of *Howard Hill: The Man and the Legend* (1982, Charger Productions Inc.), allowed me to use photographs from his book. Doyen John Schulz, author of *Hitting 'em like Howard Hill* and *Straight Shooting*, also permitted me to use parts of his publications. Bob Wesley's *Traditional Archery Adventures* and Don Carson's *Early Adventures with Howard Hill*, published by Ted Fry, are very interesting books, too. Ted Fry provided me with helpful material on Hill.

Louis Higham's *Errol Flynn, The Untold Story*, is another good book for all those who want to learn more about the "Greatest Archer of the World."

Of course, one has to watch movies or short films featuring Hill, and even watch sequences in slow-motion, to catch a glimpse of his talent and shooting style. *The Complete Archery Book*, by Louis Hochman, is a fine book with chapters such as "Bow Hunting with Howard Hill" and "Howard Hill, World's Greatest Bow Hunter." Fred Anderson's observations regarding Hill, George Brommers' quips in *Ye Sylvan Archer*, and various chapters in Bob Swinehart's and Bill Negley's books helped me become familiar with Hill, his life, and his era.

Apart from Howard's popular hunting adventures, sometimes disapproved of today, one might take a critical stance towards him. Some people held a grudge against Howard Hill because he made a living out of shooting the bow and making films. They said he was a fake, just a Hollywood invention. Of course, some of Hill's contemporaries were as good as Hill, and it was not Hill alone who "invented" the Hill-style bow; and it was definitely not OK to say that it was impossible to shoot a recurve bow under hunting conditions (it would be unfair to doubt Bill Negley's trophies from Africa).

Let's get a closer look at Howard Hill. We can assume that someone practicing four hours every day, shooting thousands of arrows, and when not practicing, spending every other day in his life bowhunting, was an excellent archer. And everyone personally acquainted with Hill confirms that.

Some people believed, and some still believe today, that Hill was a purely instinctive archer. But that's wrong. He was always in best form because he practiced every day. He seemed to shoot easily and effortlessly; one might think Howard only had to fix a target visually in order to hit it. But watching Hill's films, studying his shooting style, one thing becomes clear—he hit a target simply because he was Howard Hill, he was just a natural talent; and that's why there is not need to rack our brains over how he managed to do it. In particular, when shooting at moving targets, he effortlessly changed his anchor point and draw length.

Hill used a kind of point of aim system. He picked an imaginary point where the tip of the arrow should be in relation to his target. He called it split-vision-method. Constant practice was the basis of his incredible shots at moving targets, whether he was trick shooting or bowhunting; but we could also attribute them to instinctive shooting. With 60-pounders, plus or minus one inch in draw length will not affect a well-released shot from nine to sixteen yards. The arrow is propelled forwards and does not fall down over that distance.

Fred Anderson and Craig Ekin reported an interesting story that they learned from Frank Eicholtz. At an archery meet in San Diego, California, Hill went around and got an arrow or two from each archer—men, women, youngster, and. Those arrows, more than 50, less than 100, were of various weights, lengths, and spine values. Hill shot all of those arrows at a cardboard box which he had put on a tree 30 yards away. It was a fine group of arrows within a circle of twelve inches.

Image 79. Flight-shooting

In his *Traditional Archery Adventures and Tips*, Bob Wesley thoroughly explains Hill's shooting style.

Everyone agrees that Hill was a very good, incredibly strong athlete with considerable body control. He could have also made a career as a golf or football pro. Bows of a 100 pounds and more were his tools of trade. Shooting a 172-pounder he set a new flight record of 391 yards, 1 foot, 11 inches on February 26, 1928, in Miami, Florida.

Howard set records in every branch of archery—flight, target, or field—but it was his well-documented success as a hunter that gained him worldwide fame. Hill took more game with the bow and arrow than any other hunter before him. He was a masterful stalker, a master in ground hunting. In regards to bowhunting I want to add the following—no one should get the wrong image of bowhunting when watching videos or hearing stories. Hunting with the bow, above all stalking, is difficult and fair. Wild animals, with their sharp instincts, senses, fast speed, out match every hunter.

Like Fred Bear, Howard Hill knew how to handle the media. He did advertise-

Image 80. Bob Wesley

ments for Chesterfield (Ligett & Morris Tobacco Co.), Gilette (The Gilette Company), and various bowmaking companies. He toured through the US, performed in theaters, and advertised his films and Hill products. He marketed himself as the "World's Greatest Archer."

Howard Hill epitomized the spirit of his era. He lectured in schools, wrote books, and made short movies with Warner Brothers. Through the film *Robin Hood* he was acquainted with Jack Warner and Errol Flynn. The Tasmanian Errol Flynn was an adventurer and a swashbuckler in real life. As long as it was crazy and dangerous enough for him, it was easy to pique Flynn's interest. Howard Hill and Errol Flynn were good friends until Flynn's early death.

Back in those days I believe people loved fellows like Howard Hill, a good-looking guy, an adventurer who knew how to ride and shoot, who fought wild beasts on safaris, and who, at the same time, was fun to be with, courageous, and a champ.

There are countless, unforgettable anecdotes and stories about Hill's masterly shots—killing a wapiti over 185 yards, splitting the arrow in *Robin Hood,* shooting the stuntmen off their horses, winning 196 tourneys in a row, or shooting a 172-pounder—that was Ol' One Shot-Hill.

There was something special about Howard Hill. He knew the right people, that's what John Lee believes. As early as 1933, before *Robin Hood* (1938), Ned Frost made the nature film *The Last Wilderness,* starring Ol' One-Shot, Howard Hill. Among other things, Hill is shown bagging a buffalo "Western-style"—riding a horse at full gallop. The film is available on DVD.

However, Ned Frost, later reported that Hill was not able to shoot the buffalo from horseback. This is referenced in the 1984 book *Tracks, Trails, and Tales: The Legacy of Ned,* by Dick Frost. Hill tried but was unable to pull off shooting a buffalo riding a bareback horse. So Hill shot a buffalo from the ground, mounted his horse and rode up to the downed buffalo and dismounted. Frost filmed it and it looked like they wanted it to for the picture—and that's the footage we have. So, we can see, not all of Hill's feats were done properly. But anybody who has tried to do

Image 81. Cody Roiter of Michigan, shooting in perfect Hill-style.

some stunt or trick in front of a camera knows that things don't always happen as we'd like them to as the film is running. Time is money, even in the old days.

Despite the "special effects" of movies like *The Last Wilderness,* this kind of action or blood sport was extremely popular. Hemingway never got tired of publicly praising the beauty of bullfights. People were excited. That kind of macho image was popular, above all, among men, at least from the Stone Age until the end of the '60s. Even today, the magic of that era is working on us—we all like to watch these old adventure movies starring Bogart, Gary Cooper, John Wayne, or Jimmy Stewart.

Image 82. *Hunting the Hard Way*, illustration by Raymond Naylor.

Everyone who knew him described Howard Hill as an honest family man who loved children, although he and Elizabeth never had any children of their own. Howard never turned away any youth interested in archery.

However, if people got too close, Hill could be very reserved, he was very protective about his private life. True friends were always welcome to have a coffee or a coke in his workshop, while chatting expertly about archery. Contemporaries say that he loved to play tricks on people he liked.

Howard never wore any camouflage clothes, he usually said, "The Lord gave that bobcat some funny colors, but he eats purty regular—and if it works for him, by golly, it'll work for you!" Hill only wore plaid hunting shirts. This might be thought-provoking for bowhunters who stress having the latest hunting clothes, their faces painted black, and their bodies bathed in the latest "Doe-Odor-for-He-Men-in-Heat-Fox-Urine" products. These are the hunters who think the back quiver is useless for hunting and that straight-ended longbows are just a level above a slingshot. I think today we like to make use of any product or philosophy available as not to miss any chance during a hopefully successful hunting trip, which costs us a fortune. Anything that helps could be decisive for success or failure. Hill did not need any modern gimmicks or gadgets. Maybe the game population was

Image 83. Two champions: Ann Marston and Howard Hill.

higher and the pressure to hunt successfully lower. Maybe there was one important aspect that he handled in a different manner. Some believe it was his aftershave. Well, and he smoked.

At camp, he was always the first to get up before dawn and make coffee, unless some of his hunting chums had lost a bet the day before and had to do it. He was always clean shaven, proud to be a gentleman hunter. John Schulz wrote that whether he was stalking a rabbit or a desired trophy, he always displayed the same patience and carefulness. In *Hunting the Hard Way* Howard describes his almost perfect stalking method. Having observed lynxes and other predators, he tried to imitate their wary stalking method when hunting other animals. It is said that he learned some of his other methods while hunting with Native Americans.

Due to his impressive personality and his tremendous influence on archery, Howard's name will remain unforgettable. Appearing in movies, radio shows, and on TV, he reached myriad people with his tricks and his books. Lots of people started shooting the bow and arrow because of him. Worldwide, Howard Hill was the first archer to be honored in the US Sports Hall of Fame, next to football and baseball stars. There is still much to be told about the World's Greatest Archer.

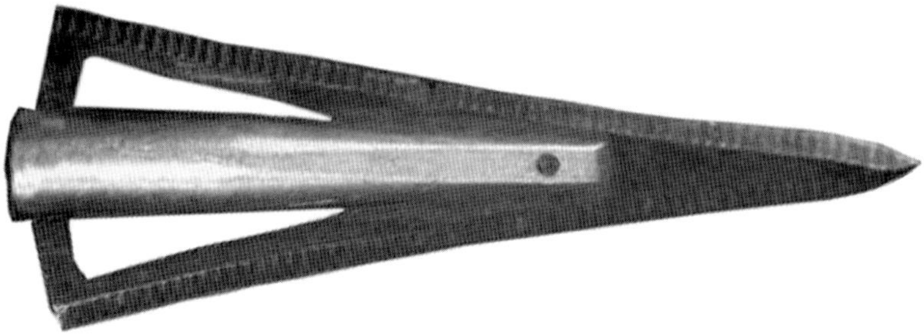

Image 84. Hill broadhead

Howard Hill may be seen as the patron saint of today's straight-ended longbow hardliners. Nothing can stop them on September 13, Howard's birthday. They stumpshoot like Hill and shoot around camp like Ol' One Shot loved to do—shooting for speed, as Howard used to say. Sometimes they shoot at paper plates thrown into the air by a courageous comrade. They shoot arrows over ditches, canyons, or into rivers, paying tribute to old Howard. They play like kids. Yes, that's true and I believe there are worse traditions.

"When the buffalo are gone, we will hunt mice, for we are hunters and want our freedom," as Sitting Bull put it. Howard Hill often claimed Native American ancestry. I believe he had some of Sitting Bull's spirit in him. Even more than his shooting skills, we should admire the passion he felt for archery.

Howard Hill died on February 4, 1975, in Vincent, Alabama. His wife, Elizabeth "Libba" Hodges Hill died eighteen months later.

They are in Valhalla, where all legends in archery dwell—eternally.

In 2009, Craig Ekin told me a fact about Howard Hill that I did not know. In his last will and testament, Howard had donated most of his archery stuff to North American Indians. The gear was auctioned and the proceeds went to the Indians.

A very humble display of altruism from the World's Greatest Archer, in my opinion.

References:
Howard Hill, *Hunting the Hard Way*
Howard Hill, *Wild Adventure*
Bob Swinehart, *Sagittarius*
Bill Negley, *Archer in Africa*
Craig Ekin, *Howard Hill: The Man and the Legend*
Bob Wesley, *Traditional Archery Adventures and Tips for Better Shooting*
Don Carson, *Early Adventures with Howard Hill*
John Schulz, *Hitting 'em like Howard Hill*
John Schulz, *Straight Shooting*
Byron Ferguson, *Become the Arrow*
Louis Hochham, *The Complete Archery Book*
Fred Anderson, *The Traditional Way: The Mystique and Heritage of Archery*
Charles Higham, *Errol Flynn: The untold Story*
J.A. Davis, *Ye Sylvan Archer*

My thanks to John D. Lee, Cliff Huntington, John Schulz, Craig Ekin, Ted Fry, Nate Steen, Bob Wesley, and Cody Roiter who helped me through personal correspondence to adequately present the archer Howard Hill.

William Negley

William Negley

Image 85. Bill Negley

Today, not too many archers know who Bill Negley is. One reason for this could be that he did not market or advertise his adventures like Howard Hill, Ben Pearson, or Fred Bear did. We should not forget that the fame Hill and Bear enjoyed was dependent on trick shooting, archery tackle sold under their names, films, and books.

Things were quite different for Mr. Negley, a lawyer and very successful businessman from Texas, who was independently wealthy. For him, archery and bowhunting were a sport, a hobby; the bow and arrow were tools for hunting, not a passion.

I first heard of (and saw) Bill Negley when I was watching a video of Fred Bear's film, *Moments of Truth*. Negley, armed with a 102-pound recurve, and only one arrow in his hand, was stalking a bull elephant in Africa's long grass.

William Negley was born on March 26, 1914, in San Antonio, Texas. He died in his hometown on November 9, 2006. In between he had a very interesting life. After attending law school, he practiced law until 1942, when he volunteered for military service. Upon his discharge, Negley, with the help of his father-in-law, founded a paper bag manufacturing plant. Mr. Negley was married to Carolyn Brown from 1942 until 1958. Then, in 1977, Mr. Negley married Lolly Carrigan Fitzsimons. He spent many happy years with her until her death in 1993. Mr. Negley was an enthusiastic hunter, fisherman, and nature conservationist. In later life Mr. Negley devoted much of his time working on the conservation and protection of fish, shrimp, and crabs in the bays of Texas. In 2000 he was named Conservationist of the Year by the Texas Parks and Wildlife Commission.

Image 86. Hunting elephants.

Throughout his life, William Negley was a rifle hunter and deep-sea fisher, but he gradually lost interest in hunting with the rifle. It was just too easy, too precise for Bill. He explained why: He had just taught his daughter, aged eight, how to shoot, when she bagged a whitetail from over 100 meters. In the following year she again shot a whitetail buck from more than 120 meters. When he asked her if she wanted to go hunting with him, she said no. Negley believed that his daughter, in three short years, had gained an insight that had taken him twenty-five years to reach.

Well, within three years, his daughter not only learned how to handle a rifle effectively, but also lost her interest in hunting.

To give up hunting completely was not in Negley's interest and so he took to the bow and arrow more and more each day. Shooting the bow was always a challenge for him, no matter how many months or how hard he practiced. This is an aspect of our marvelous sport that we all know well. Hitting a target at 25 meters with a bow is quite different from hitting a target at 200 meters with a good gun equipped with an optical gadget.

Today, Bill Negley's book, *Archer in Africa*, is very rare and usually sold, if at all, for more than $400. It is a beautiful, leather-bound book with gilded letters and a slipcase. Amwell Press published it in 1989 as volume 24 of the *African Hunting Heritage Collection*. It was printed in an limited edition run of 1,000 copies. In 1995 I had no clue at all how precious the book was when I bought a copy for $100 from Joe St. Charles's *Northwest Archery* catalog. At the time, $100 seemed like a lot of money, especially when the catalog had no pictures of the book and the only description listed was, "Bill Negley left us some copies. As it turned out, however, the volume was signed by Bill Negley, and today I am happy I got hold of the book.

The story behind *Archer in Africa* began in June 1956, at the Cat Cay yacht port in the Bahamas. The Bahamas had always been a favorite meeting place for wealthy deep-sea fishers trying to catch fish schools moving north. In spring there were shoals of huge bluefin tuna moving north, from the Caribbean to the coastal waters of Long Island, Maine, Nova Scotia, and the Prince Edward's Islands on to the high seas of the North Atlantic. In late fall, the fish headed back south into the Caribbean. In the evenings the fishers met at the Yacht Club, talked about that day's catch and planned the next hunting or fishing season. At such a meeting, Bill Carpenter of Wilmington, Delaware, asked Bill Negley for his hunting plans for the near future.

Image 87. A Fred Bear 107-pounder.

Negley had recently come back from an African safari with his friend Laurence Wood from southern Texas. They had shot quite a quarry of big game with their hunters, Bunny Allen and Norman Read. Negley had a keen interest in elephant hunts—an inclination that is hard or almost impossible to explain to non-hunters.

I would not be very interested in hunting elephants today, but things were quite different in the 1950s. Even today, there are many controversial points of view. Painting it in black-and-white, the bad hunter and the good animal rights activist, we will, as usual, not come up with a relevant view.

Even though animal welfarists might throw up their hands in horror, it is necessary, even today, to shoot a certain amount of these nice animals, due to a limited habitat on one hand and a growing number of elephants on the other hand. There are also programs limiting the number of animals through castration. Whereas these programs for reducing the elephant population cost quite some money, selling licenses for shooting elephants is quite profitable for the National Parks. The profits made are then used for protecting and improving the living conditions of the wild animals. At least, that's what should be done.

That there is less and less natural habitat for elephants is not the fault of the bad hunter; one should rather blame this on the agricultural usage or tourism. Poaching has been a problem for quite some time. But ever since rigid measures (automatic weapons) have been taken against poachers, it looks like they are the ones in danger of becoming extinct. One could fill books with this topic. But as this is impossible for me given the scope of this book, this was just a short safari into the world of animal protection and habitat conservation.

Eventually Negley recognized bow hunting as an alternative hunting method. At 38, he had almost given up on hunting with the rifle and he was hunting with a pistol. Again, a hunting method too easy for Bill. A business associate from Wisconsin first told Negley about hunting deer with bow and arrow. Bill remembered the Robin Hood games of his childhood. Soon after he heard of Fred Bear. In French Equatorial Africa, Fred had successfully taken antelopes with the bow and arrow. A few years earlier, Howard Hill made his safari film, *Tembo,* in the Belgian Congo, bagging an elephant with his longbow.

But back to Cat Cay in the Bahamas. While they were drinking cocktails, Bill explained his objections to rifle hunting and his interest in more serious things. In the two years leading up to that conversation, he had done a fair amount of hunting with the bow and arrow.

The fishers and hunters present could not believe that Bill had taken to such an inefficient weapon and form of hunting. This initiated a debate and Bill announced that he was planning a safari trip to Africa for the following year, 1957, to hunt with the bow and arrow. He would like to take big game, and maybe an elephant, with the bow. This declaration precipitated a moment of quiet appraisal, followed by polite disbelief among his comrades. Mr. Carpenter asked Bill politely why he thought it possible to take an elephant with the bow and arrow, surely this was an impossible feat. Negley mentioned Howard Hill, and although he would not be as excellent archer as Hill, he was certain of being a good hunter. They were idly chatting until Bill Carpenter said that Howard Hill only managed to kill an elephant after a white hunter had shot it in the knee, otherwise it would not have been possible to film it. Therefore, he was sure that an arrowed elephant would disappear into the wilds.

Image 88. Howard Hill, 1949.

Negley countered that Hill's arrow had certainly killed the elephant, believing it possible to bag the thick-skinned animal armed only with a bow—without the help of rifles. This would be a legal bow trophy and a fair way to take an elephant.

"Well, Bill," Mr. Carpenter answered. "If you think you can do it, I'll bet 10,000 dollars against it. If you lose, you'll give me 1,000 dollars."

"OK, I'll see if I get a permit for this kind of hunt and I'll let you know when the bet is on," Bill Negley said to Carpenter.

Image 89. October 31: lion. The Big Five were complete.

Today, it would be a wager of $100,000 to $10,000. Obviously these guys didn't worry about money. By the way, Bill won the bet and donated the money to charity.

Bill got in touch with companies arranging hunting safaris in Africa, such as Ker & Downey of Nairobi, Kenya, Eric Rundgren in Tanganjika, and others. But in most countries hunting with the bow was not permitted for various reasons. There were some funny arguments against it. Those responsible for hunting thought if they permitted bowhunting in traditional safari countries, they would ruin the glamour and the classical image of big game hunting and have to slash the prices. How would they explain the presence of men armed with toy-like hunting gear taking the Big Five from short range to all those wealthy hunters who were taking their trophies with heavy caliber rifles, backed by professional white hunters? The familiar macho image of Robert Ruarks, Ernest Hemingways, and others would gradually be ruined and need a new definition. No, this was not the purpose of a safari.

Image 90. White hunter and author Peter Hathaway Capstick.

Negley was absolutely right in believing that any game bagged with a bow, but kneecapped with a rifle, could not count as a bow trophy. Bill Negley wanted to know where Carpenter had heard of this knee-shooting story and found out that Hill's camp while filming *Tembo* in the Belgian Congo was only two or three miles from Carpenter's hunting camp. Every evening at dusk, Hill's professional hunters and his cameraman had a few drinks at Carpenter's camp. Hill was, according to what his team said about him, an early-to-bed-early-to-rise fellow, and there was never any alcohol at his camp. While Howard was sound asleep, the cameraman and the hunters were enjoying a relaxing evening after an exhausting day. They were chatting idly, and this is how Carpenter learned about the lesser-known details of Howard Hill's elephant hunt. It's not a nice story, but it's not entirely a work of fiction. Presumably, with the filming technique in those days, such a film could not have been made in any other way. In Hollywood films steel ropes were used to make horses fall and *Tembo* was more an adventure film than a hunting documentary.

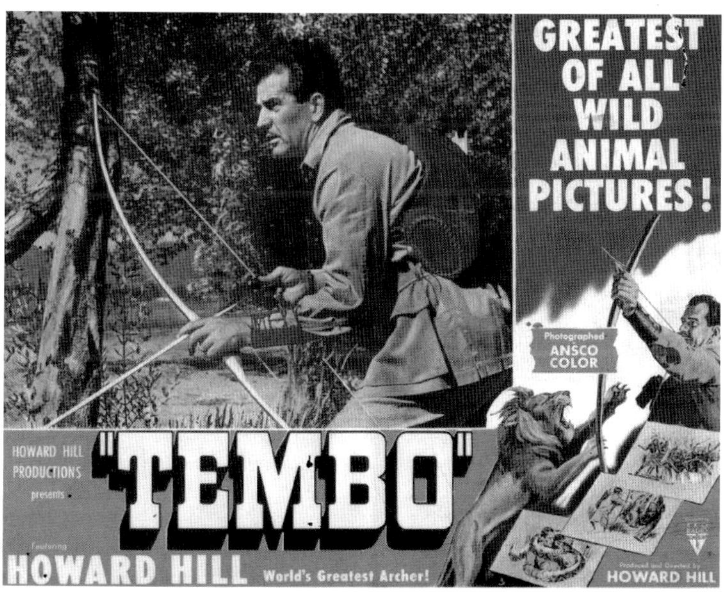

Image 91. *Tembo* movie poster.

As far as I know, one could not say that Bill Negley and Howard Hill were comrades. In a hunting magazine Hill said that it was impossible to take elephants with Negley's equipment. Negley responded by asking Hill to accompany him on his next safari. Hill turned that offer down, pretending he had not meant it that way.

So, we come to the mysteries and rumors surrounding taking the Big Five with a bow and arrow. In October 1966, several years after the bet in the Bahamas, Negley was on a safari in Angola. By then, he had already taken the Big Five without the help of a rifle. In November, when he stopped at the Continental Hotel in Luanda to organize his trip back, Jorge Alves de Lima, Bill's professional hunter, handed him the local evening newspaper. US-bowhunter Bob Swinehart was said to have taken a lion in Mozambique, being the first white man to bag the Big Five.

Bill had not known that Swinehart, too, was on a safari. He found out that Swinehart, accompanied by professional hunter Rui Almeida, had already begun hunting in Angola in June. On July 4, he bagged the lion in Mozambique, completing his Big Five with the bow and arrow—about 60 days before Negley began his safari. Bob was definitely the first. When Swinehart arrived in San Antonio in 1971, he visited the Game Conservation International Convention, headed by Bill Negley, who welcomed Swinehart and helped him advertise his auspicious book, *Sagittarius*. It wasn't until 1983, when Negley met Bert Klineburger, a renowned outfitter of anything needed for a safari or polar bear hunt, and the Portuguese hunting guide, Adelino Serres Pires, that Bill Negley first doubted Swinehart's hunting exploits. Negley learned that Pires was the hunting apprentice that had accompanied Mike

Image 92. Eric Rundgren, Bill Negley, and trackers Duo and Kaveca.

Image 93. Rhino

Coelho and Bob Swinehart to Mozambique when Bob bagged the elephant. They were idly chatting about various hunting adventures and Negley's successful elephant hunt in 1957 when Bill explained that he, quite contrary to the hunt for Howard Hill's film, had taken the elephant without the help of a rifle hunter. Hearing this, Pires said that Swinehart had bagged the elephant Hill-style.

Bill Negley raised this issue in his book, disbelieving what he saw in the photos of Swinehart's elephants and rhinos. Bill, being an experienced hunter, found that Bob's arrows showed a peculiar penetration angle and depth.

Anyone interested in finding out more should read Bill Negley's *Archer in Africa*, Howard Hill's *Wild Adventure*, Craig Ekin's *Howard Hill: The Man and the Legend*, and Bow Swinehart's *Sagittarius* and *In Africa*. Read the truth between the lines with a critical eye.

I like Bill Negley's book, he wrote about failures and media criticism of his deeds, and therefore, I believe he was telling the truth. Everybody who has hunted once knows that it is not always a picture perfect fairy tale, even though some try to make us believe it.

If I ever go to San Antonio, Texas, I will visit the Buckhorn Saloon. I want to drink a glass of beer in honor of the hunter William Negley and get a closer look at his trophies, bows, and arrows, which are on display.

The following is Negley's obituary from the *New York Times*:

NEGLEY—William died November 7, 2006 in San Antonio, Texas. He was born in San Antonio on March 28, 1914 to Laura Burleson Negley and Richard Van Wyck Negley. He attended primary school in San Antonio and was graduated from Phillips Exeter Academy in 1932. He received a Bachelor of Arts degree from the University of Texas in 1935, attended the University of Texas Law School and was admitted to the Texas Bar Association in 1937. He practiced law with the Standard Oil Company of New Jersey in the United States and Venezuela until he volunteered for military service in 1942. Upon discharge he founded, with the help of his father-in-law Lutcher Brown, a paper bag manufacturing plant in Monroe, Louisiana. He sold the company to Olin Mathison in 1957 and started a business developing lots and building homes in San Antonio. Some years later he was asked by his father, Richard Negley, to take over management of the Negley Paint Company. He did and operated it very successfully until it was sold in 1985. Mr. Negley was married to Carolyn Brown from 1942 until 1958. In 1977 Mr. Negley married Lolly Carrigan Fitzsimons and spent many happy years with her until her death in 1993. Mr. Negley's two brothers, Albert and Richard were killed in World War II. Mr. Negley is survived by three children, Laura Negley Gill, James Lutcher Negley and Richard Burleson Negley; ten grandchildren, Christopher Burleson Gill, Carolyn Gill French, Josephine Gill Davidson, Richard Negley Gill, Emily Negley Martin, Nancy Negley Krissoff, Sydney Negley Mulder, William Waters Negley, Jamie Lutcher Negley and Suzanne Clementine Negley; four great-grandchildren, Laura Wells French, Adele Burleson Davidson, Henry Walling Martin and Amelia Gill French. He was also a loving and enthusiastic step-father to Pamela Fitzsimons Howard, Hugh A. Fitzsimons, III and Joseph B.C. Fitzsimons and step-grandfather of Anson Boulware Howard, Laura Isabel Howard, Louisa Carrigan Fitzsimons Howard, Hugh A. Fitzsimons, IV, Patrick Carrigan Fitzsimons and Evelyn Bailey Fitzsimons, Fay Carrigan Fitzsimons, Jonathan Calvert Fitzsimons and Katherine Burgwin Fitzsimons.Throughout his life Mr. Negley was an enthusiastic hunter, fisherman and conservationist. He was captain of the last United States team to fish in the International Tuna Match in Nova Scotia and held several fly rod and bow hunting world records. He was the first and only bow hunter to take buffalo, elephant, black rhino, leopard and lion with no rifle protection. In later life Mr. Negley spent a great deal of his time working on the conservation and protection of the fish, shrimp and crabs of the bays of Texas. He was an early and strong supporter of the concept of buying out the rights of commercial harvesters of shrimp, crabs and finfish in order to protect those assets for the recreational use of the general public. Mr. Negley was a life board member of the Coastal Conservation Association and in 2000 was named Conservationist of the Year by the Texas Parks and Wildlife Commission. A memorial service will be held at Christ Church, 510 Belknap, San Antonio on Friday, November 10 at 1:30 PM. Contributions in lieu of flowers may be sent to Phillips Exeter Academy or the Texas Parks and Wildlife Foundation.

Image 94. T.J. Conrads, publisher of *Traditional Bowhunter Magazine,* and Bill Negley.

References:
Bob Swinehart, *Sagittarius*
Bob Swinehart, *In Africa*
Bill Negley, *Archer in Africa*
New York Times, November 9, 2006

Bob Swinehart

Bob Swinehart

Image 95. Bob Swinehart

Bob Swinehart's books, *In Africa* and *Sagittarius,* are two of the most wanted bow and arrow classics.

Both books are about hunting African big game with the bow and arrow. Most books dealing with that subject are rare due to their limited print runs and the growing number of book collectors. Everyone collecting antiquarian bow and arrow books connects with bowhunting somehow. A reason for this is that until the 1970s, any form of hunting was more acceptable. Fred Bear's hunting films were shown in a positive light at American cinemas. Today, this would raise the protests of animal-rights activists and the media.

Authors documenting their hunting trips were children in their time, just like us today. Being a macho man was popular when Ernest Hemingway was writing *Death in the Afternoon* and *Green Hills of Africa,* literature that is not suitable for thin-skinned, sensitive people.

Bob Swinehart was born in Pottstown, Pennsylvania, in 1928. There are many descendents of German and Dutch settlers in this region, which explains his love of salted pretzels. In many photos of Swinehart a huge box of salted pretzels is ubiquitous.

Bob Swinehart was definitely one of Howard Hill's followers, using straight-ended longbows made of bamboo, backed and faced with fiberglass, and the obligatory, roomy back quiver. During the 1960s, lots of archers shot the new Micro-flite arrows, which were tapered, hollow fiberglass arrows. Swinehart use both wooden arrows and these new ones. Sometimes he used the recurve instead of the longbow, for example, a Ben Pearson bushmaster, and aluminum arrows.

In his foreword to *Sagittarius*, Howard Hill describes Swinehart as a patient and unpretentious hunter, and as an extraordinary trick shot, who, like Hill himself, was able to hit coins in mid-air. Standing only five feet nine inches, Bob Swinehart was rather heavily built, easily able to shoot bows drawing more than 100 pounds, even from rather unusual positions. Bob was left-handed.

Image 96. Bob's back quiver, with a file for sharpening broadheads, and leather tackle.

Hill only criticized Bob's almost foolish courage. When a journalist asked him, "How good is this guy, Swinehart?" Hill answered, "Just the greatest I ever hunted with. He'll kill the Big Five if he doesn't get himself killed first—he is too gutty for his own good!"

Image 97. "My personal reason for any kind of actual hunting is challenge, no matter what the animal or weapon." Bob Swinehart in *Sagittarius*.

We should, however, bear in mind that Howard and Bob were friends. They had met in the 1950s and were advertising archery equipment for Ted Ekin's *Howard Hill Archery*, a company selling and making archery tackle under Howard's name. The Ekins, Ted's son Craig and Craig's son Jason, still run the company in Hamilton, Montana. Howard Hill bows have not changed much and are still obtainable with the same design as in the 1960s.

Howard Hill, too, was on safari in the Belgian Congo in 1950. *Tembo*, the movie about this safari, is available on video or DVD. Even today, there are lots of controversial discussions about this film, whether it is ethically justifiable. Presumably, like a lot of other movies, *Tembo* was made under the pressure of time. It was not a proper documentary, rather a movie showing lots of action, wild animals, and fearless bowhunters. Each day mattered, and if any hunting scene required more time than allowed, the whole project would have failed. This is why some of the hunting situations appear unreal. Even today, some accuse Hill of shooting at chained game. But in regard to the technical equipment at that time, it would have been impossible to make these kinds of adventure movies otherwise.

We all know the classic safari movies of the 1940s, '50s, and '60s—what a different era. There is nothing unusual about it, this was cinema back then. Steward Granger killed attacking rhinos and Clark Gable shot "bad" lions or crocodiles trying to nibble at Grace Kelly or Ava Gardner having a bath. *Tembo* should be regarded as a movie; it is not a real hunting film, not even a suitable example for bowhunting safaris.

Bob Swinehart, aspiring to be as good as his role model Howard Hill, ventured on hunting trips from Angola to Mozambique between 1964 and 1966.

Image 98. Hill and Swinehart.

Swinehart's white hunter was Rui Almeida from Portugal, whose competent support helped Swinehart bag Cape buffalo, a rhino, various kinds of gazelles, and an elephant with his 110-pound longbow. Rui Almeida was a typical white hunter, like the ones you see in those old safari movies, able to entertain his hunting guests in six languages, including two native dialects. On later safaris, Mike Coelho, also Portuguese, was Bob's hunter and backup man, the archer's life insurance. A white hunter should be able to do anything, from repairing the Land Rover to looking for dangerous game in the long grass, to organizing camp and bearing their hunting guests' whims and fancies. And, of course, they must have detailed knowledge of the animals' habits—another one of his tasks. The success or failure of a hunt trip, and the life of the guest, were in the white hunter's hands. And after an exhausting day in the wild, he even had to entertain the guests at the camp fire, drinking and chatting about the day's events, planning the next days, or telling thrilling hunting stories. It is a 24-hour job. Therefore, some of these hunters became legends. Safari aficionados should read, among other books, the works of Bror von Blixen, James Cottar, Frederick C. Selous, Denis Finch-Hatton, Philip Perceval, James Patterson, J.A. Hunter, Robert Foran, John Boyes, Jim Sutherland, James Pondero Taylor, Richard von Meinertzhagen, Karamojo Bell, Ernst A. Zwilling, Leslie Simpson, Steward Edward White, Jim Corbett, Werner von Alvensleben, and Peter H. Capstick. Their stories are definitely worth reading. They show their readers a mysterious, adventurous, thrilling, typical, dark Africa, leading them back to an era of gentlemen hunters, down-to-earth men, scholars, daredevil archers, soldiers, smugglers, writers, and athletes. An era of tropical helmets, tuxedo and champagne soirees, and elegant American ladies. An era of Hemingways, failures, half-legal ivory hunters…

Bob Swinehart left us two books. *In Africa*, a ninety-eight-page, illustrated paperback was published by Boyertown Publishing Company, Pennsylvania, in 1967. It documents four Swinehart safaris—Angola/Mozambique in 1964 and Angola/Mozambique in 1966. The Big Five, elephant, rhino, buffalo, leopard, and lion, were bagged during these trips. Swinehart claimed to be the first white bow-hunter to have achieved this feat. By 1950, Hill had taken all of the Big Five except the rhino. He was targeting one, but his backup man had to rescue him from the attacking colossus.

We already know Bill Negley's opinion the Big Five from *Archer in Africa*.

Bob Swinehart's *In Africa* is very rare, only 5,000 copies were printed and prices vary from $150 to $250. There are no plans to print a new edition.

Image 99. Professional hunter Rui Almeida.

Image 100. *In Africa*, 1967.

Sagittarius, published in 1970 by Gallant Publishing Company, Covina, California, is an abundantly illustrated, 240-page hardcover volume. If Bob Swinehart intended to leave a lasting memorial with *Sagittarius*, he really managed to do so. Outdoor painter Doug van Howd's marvelous illustrations make this book an antiquarian's delight.

The book is about Bob's childhood and youth, his first hunting adventures in America, and his friendship with longbow guru and veteran archer, Ol' One Shot, Howard Hill. One chapter is exclusively dedicated to Swinehart's equipment. And the chapter "Why hunt?" describes his thoughts on hunting. The majority of *Sagittarius* is, as *In Africa* before, dedicated to his safaris.

Sagittarius was reprinted in the 1990s as part of the Glenn St. Charles *Legends of the Longbow* series. But this edition does not live up to the original one—all the color illustrations from the first edition, as well as lots of photos, are printed in back and white.

And if you manage to acquire the original publication, the dust jacket is often missing. *Sagittarius* is sold at prices between $175 and $350 and I have seen the *Legends of the Longbow* reprints for $150.

But I was really lucky. In 1998 I ordered a few copies of *44 Years Behind The Bow* by Mr. Cliff Coe of Otter Lake, Michigan. Coe was an old time archer and his book is a unique, informative work. He was a noted bowyer in his days, producing his own broadhead, the Coe Slasher. But he did not make many heads, and today they are a very rare collector's item. I asked Mr. Coe if he knew an antiquarian bookshop where I could buy an original edition of *Sagittarius*. He said the book was out of print. I knew that much; so far I had only seen a single copy for $250. I must add that the quest for antiquarian books in the pre-Internet age was an extremely difficult and tedious task. Mr. Coe wrote that he would tell me if he came across a copy. I had almost forgotten the matter, when two years later he wrote again; he had found an

Image 101. *Sagittarius*, 1970.

original copy of *Sagittarius* with dust jacket and he knew it was worth more than $200. He said he would send it to me for $50. I quickly sent him the money, asking him to sign the book for me. Experiences like this one make collectors appreciate their rare books even more; at least that's how I feel about it.

I would like to make a special reference to Mr. Coe and thank him for his help. In 2007, while I was working on the German version of this book, Mr. Coe passed.

Back to Bob Swinehart. He was among the founding members of the Pope & Young Club and he wrote for numerous archery and hunting magazines.

From 1970 to 1974, he headed his father-in-law's company. But in 1972, Swineharts' marriage to his wife June, with whom he had two sons, ended in divorce. She remarried soon afterwards. In 1974, Bob was engaged to a woman named Catherine. They wanted to study mountain gorillas in Gabon. But soon the couple ended the relationship. It looks like they fell apart in Africa and Bob returned to Pennsylvania, where he started to suffer from depression.

After carefully studying books and newspapers and personally contacting archery historians in the US, I believe that Swinehart was striving to become as famous an archer as Howard Hill.

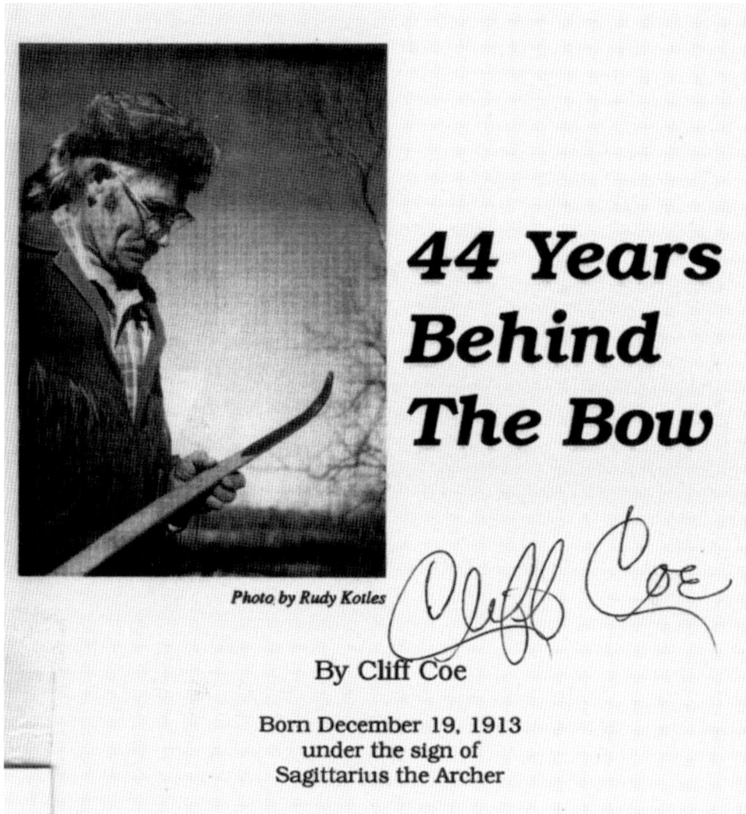

44 Years Behind The Bow

Photo by Rudy Kotles

By Cliff Coe

Born December 19, 1913
under the sign of
Sagittarius the Archer

Image 102. *44 Years Behind The Bow.*

Bob, a successful lawyer and businessman, could have had a happy life; he would not have needed any public hype. But his extreme ambitiousness made him strive for new tasks; maybe he was addicted to adrenalin, needed to get a kick out of more action. Maybe he needed adventures to escape his depression. Excuse my unprofessional attempts at psychology, I only try to write about my feelings and impressions.

In January 1982, Bob's brother David, who had made millions in real estate, was killed under suspicious circumstances. At that time Bob was working as district manager for an agricultural company in Ohio. His depression became worse and he finally needed psychotherapy. In those days that meant electroshock therapy.

Maybe an interesting parallel to note is that Ernest Hemingway, who was also suffering from depression back then, was treated with electroshock therapy at the famous Mayo clinic. Hemingway shot himself with a hunting rifle.

Image 103. Swinehart with a recurve and deadhead.

On a Monday afternoon, Bob drove to the Swinehart building previously owned by his brother. He wanted to look for some of his things that he had stored there. Among them were some of his hunting rifles. In May 1982, Robert N. Swinehart ended his adventurous life with a .243 hunting rifle. He was buried in his hometown, Pottstown, Pennsylvania. I believe Bob certainly found a place at the table with the immortal hunters, those who have departed for the happy hunting grounds.

Image 104. Hunting lions in Mozambique.

References:
Bob Swinehart, *Sagittarius*
Bob Swinehart, *In Africa*
Bill Negley, *Archer in Africa*

John Schulz

John Schulz

Image 105. John Schulz

Anyone who wants to learn more about Howard Hill and his shooting technique should read John Schulz's works *Hitting 'em like Howard Hill*, 1975, and *Straight Shooting*, published in 2002.

The books describes the friendship between the Schulz boys, Dan and John, and Hill.

After Howard's death in 1975, Elizabeth Hill wrote a foreword for *Hitting 'em like Howard Hill*, confirming John's expert knowledge of Howard Hill's equipment, shooting, and hunting methods:

> *Among the thousands of archery friends and admirers of my late husband, Howard Hill, if I were picking one to describe and explain Howard's methods in every detail, I know no one I would trust to do so correctly, fully and in detail as I do John Schulz, the author of this book about Howard. How he hunted, his methods, his every requisite in hunting and shooting are all accurately described...*

As a teenager in 1949, John Schulz heard Howard Hill lecture at Van Nuys High School in Van Nuys, California. Hill explained his plan to hunt elephants with the bow and arrow and he showed a special 1500-grain arrow with a special broadhead that he designed. He also demonstrated his longbow, Gran'ma. After this performance, John knew if there was anyone capable of bagging an elephant with a bow, then it was Mr. Hill.

Subsequently, the Hills invited Dan and John to their fine house in Pacoima, California. Howard and Elizabeth, who did not have any children themselves, liked having the Schulz boys over and Hill took John and Dan under his wings. According to John, Hill was good-humored but a strict teacher. Under his critical eyes the boys made their first bows in Hill's garage. In the backyard there was a barbecue,

Howard's favorite place in the garden, and next to it there were some sand piles and bales of straw for a backstop.

Occasionally, Hill phoned the boys, saying "Bring your bows and arrows, we're going to have a fun shoot." Howard was a member of the exclusive Toluca Lake Country Club, where he played golf with many Hollywood stars. Howard often invited movie stars, who were "ordinary" people for John and Dan, to the fun shoots. Later, when John and Dan were commercially producing archery tackle, some of these stars would be among their satisfied clients.

Dan was a better shooter, and even though he lost his right eye when unstringing his 87-pound semi-recurve bow, he still continued shooting with his right hand—truly an excellent archer. During a boar hunt, Wayne Mosley, brother of the actor Guy Madison, was standing next to Dan who bagged a strong sow with his first arrow and then the five young wild piglets that had followed the sow. Later, John Schulz asked Wayne why he had not taken one of the young ones. Shaking his head, Wayne answered that whenever he aimed at one, Dan's arrow had already zipped through it. It took Dan six arrows to take six wild pigs.

John Schulz once wrote me that due to the "dominant eye" there would be hardly any advantages for an instinctive shooter to change from right-handed to left-handed shooting, or the other way round. It would require much more practice to adjust the motor functions, and the result would not be very satisfying. Howard Hill, according to John, had a dominant left eye.

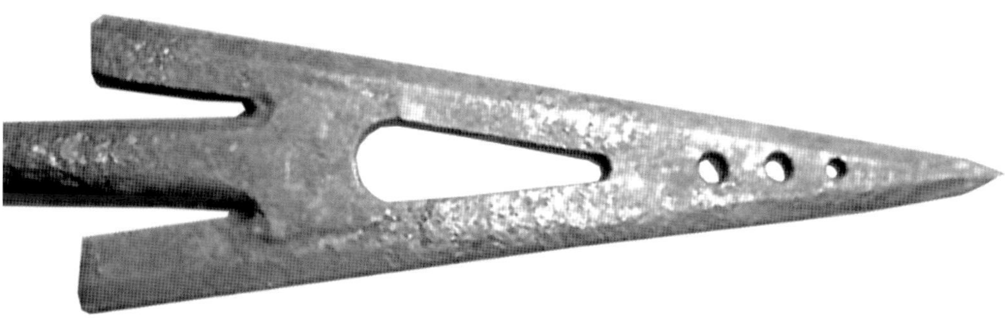

Image 106. Hill's elephant broadhead, 3.82 inches, 396 grains.

Image 107. Dan and John Schulz with Howard Hill.

Eventually, John and Dan Schulz opened LongBow Archery in Chatsworth, California, where they manufactured and sold bows under this name.

When Hill began marketing equipment for Shawnee Archery, the Schulz brothers manufactured longbows for Howard, apart from the finish. Howard signed the bows, then they were varnished and the handle leather was applied. In recent years, many of these bows have been traded as built by Howard himself. But Dan and John made these Hill-bows, Howard only looked them over and signed them. Except for a few friends, Howard did not make any bows after closing his shop in North Hollywood. The glassed bows that Dan and John made cost $50 in 1957.

A short time after opening LongBow Archery, Dan got a good job, leaving John to continue with the bow making. Towards the end of the 1950s, John settled down near Redding in Northern California. Dan Schulz died in 1986.

John changed the name of his products to American LongBow and during the 1970s he manufactured Howard Hill bows for the Ekins' company, Howard Hill Archery.

A few years ago I was in touch with Mr. Angelo Christiano of Montana, owner of BisonGear. He makes high-quality, extremely durable woolen bags and backpacks. Mr. Christiano offered me three bows—Hill-style bows previously owned by Paul "Too Short" Brunner who had been gripped by the reflex deflex fever. Two of them were American LongBow bows (66" long, 72#@26" and 74#@26") made by John Schulz, a good friend of Paul Brunner's. The third bow was a Howard Hill Archery bow (64" 66#@26") also made by John Schulz. After consulting my friend Theo Schett from Salzburg, Austria, I bought the three bows. I kept Ram Killer, the Howard Hill bow and Medicine Ram, one of the two American LongBow bows. Theo kept the third one, Ram Stalker.

They are marvelous bows, slender, made of bamboo lams, backed and faced with brown fiberglass and a myrtle wood handle. Angelo also offered me some of his Hunter's Head broadheads designed by John Schulz. I was happy to buy these as they are now very rare broadheads.

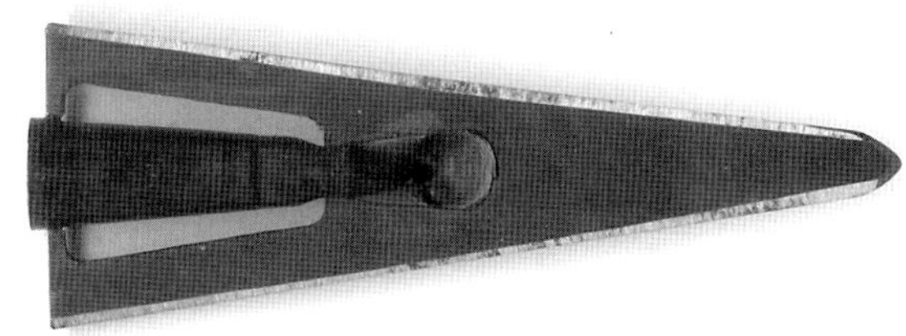

Image 108. John Schulz's Hunter's Head, 152 grains.

John Schulz was also offering bowmaking courses for a while. Some of his students' bows are very much in demand. I have a Timberline model Safari by Pete George (66" 56# @27'), an extremely accurate, comfortable bow with a light string follow. Pete George offered all his bows in a "forgiving accurate, Hill string follow limb" design or the "speed to burn, Schulz superfast reflex" design.

In *Straight Shooting*, John Schulz explains that it had taken him almost 30 years to understand one of Howard Hill's simple principles. Ever since using fiberglass, Howard, according to John, was suffering from the speed virus. He wanted more "meow"—Hill's word for speed—for his personal bows. John liked to build these fast reflex bows. When these bows were finished, they usually had too much "click," or hand-shock, for the masterly archer. Hill, always preaching that it was easier to shoot a slower bow, often used bows with a strong back set for the sake of speed; but not always, as John realized when watching Hill's movie Tembo, when Howard shot string-follow longbows. During the 1990s, John began to implement this principle, offering "naturals," made of yew, bamboo, or white oak laminates without fiberglass. Theo Schett, who has visited Schulz in Cody, Wyoming, owns one of these bows, a bamboo laminate Tonkin that John made for him. Very rare items today, Theo's bow costs $700.

Recently, US bowyers have begun applying the string-follow design of old Hill-style bows. Nate Steen of Twin Falls, Idaho, is one of them. He makes glassed longbows with slight string-follow. His Sunset Hill longbow comprises the comfortable shooting features of a self bow and the performance and stability of a good glassed longbow.

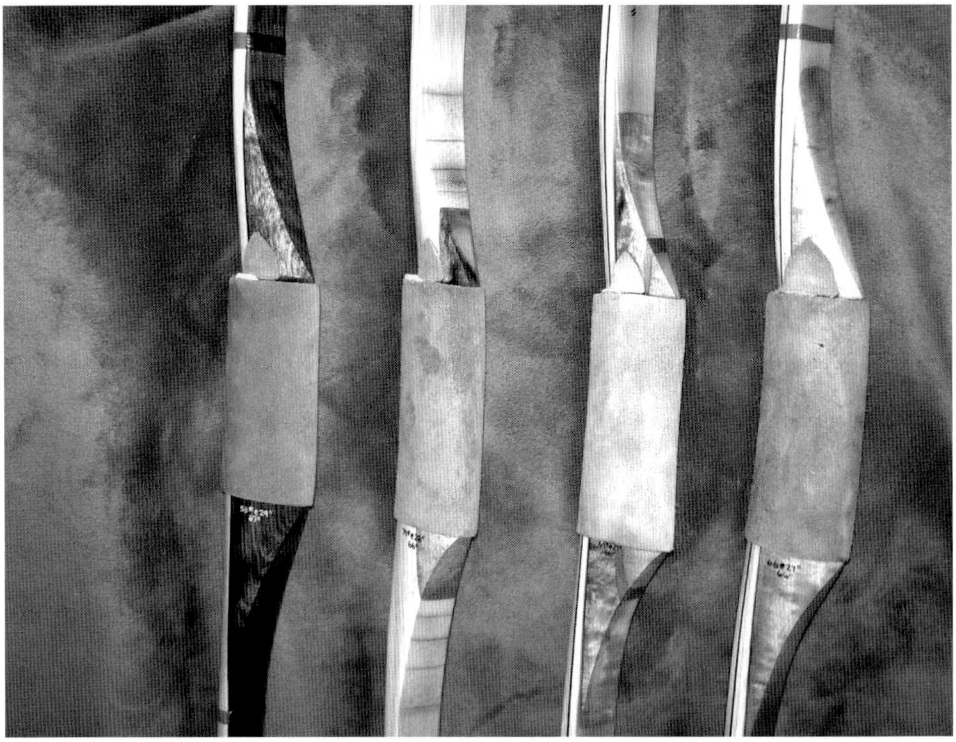

Image 109. Works of art by Nate Steen, Twin Falls, Idaho.

Ever since I first shot Nate's bow, it has been my first choice. The bow (66" 64# @27") is made of bamboo lams, it draws smoothly, and there is almost no stacking. It is a sweet shooting bow. I shoot it with a Fast Flight string and cedar wood arrows weighing at least 550 grains. It tolerates various spines without any difficulties. It is easily maneuverable and excuses one or the other technical errors.

Image 110. Homemade Hill-style back quiver.

James Schulz, one of John's sons, runs American Leathers, a shop making high-quality archery tackle. Quivers are modeled after one of Hill's quivers. John, who had to repair Howard's quivers, when, for example, the lacing had come lose, took one of Howard's favorite ones apart and copied the pattern. There are some secrets revolving around Hill's seemingly simple back quivers, but it is easy to make them. I have made some of them, too. If you have to choose between two adequate kinds of thick leather, you should choose the softer one. A functional back quiver should be broken in, it should adjust to the archer's back to make sure no arrows are spilled on the ground when the archer is bending forward. The strap should be fastened flexibly with laces so that it is easier to adjust the quiver, fixing it under the archer's armpit. This is helpful when you have to maneuver quietly and quickly. Hill always used a back quiver when he was hunting, which is in line with his stalking principle, "...if you're too loud—you're movin' too fast."

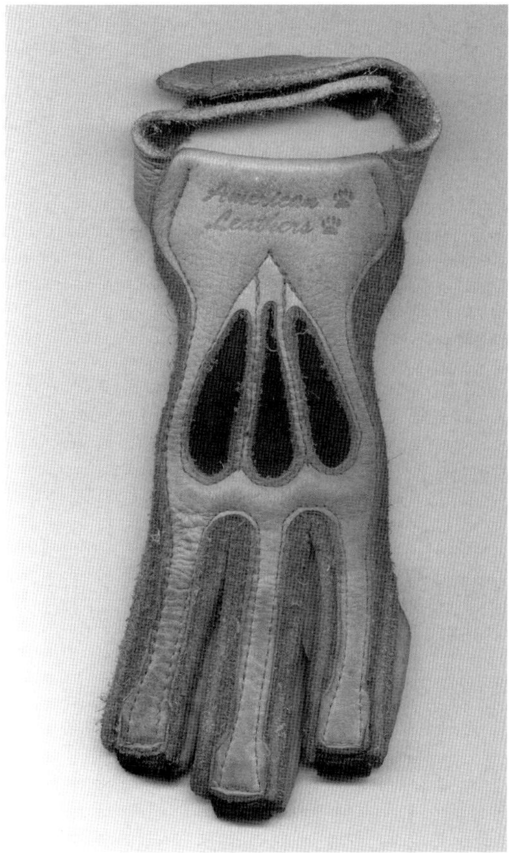

111. American Leathers' Big Shot glove.

James Schulz makes premium shooting gloves, too. They can be tailor-made to fit the client's hand. I have two different styles, both with a perfect fit. A new design is the Big Shot, which is similar to a classic deerskin glove. It is made of wapiti or buffalo hide and has an elastic neoprene lining on the back and nylon strips at the drawing side of the fingers. The glove, which is handcrafted for a high-quality, comfortable fit is also a fast glove. You can comfortably shoot heavy bows with it. Regardless of whether the glove is wet or dry, the release remains consistent. At the moment I am only using the Big Shot.

John Schulz is a master, a guardian of straight, traditional shooting. Certainly, he knows the style of archery veteran Howard Hill. With his books and seminars he keeps the spirit of the Hill-style alive for future generations.

Bob Wesley wrote in his book, *Traditional Archery Adventures and Tips for Better Shooting:*

> *I salute John Schulz for the positive image he has given traditional archery and the many other contributions he has made. His book,* Straight Shooting, *is a must read for all traditional archers. Chapter three of this book, Days in Saticoy, gives a special insight into the wonderful persona of Howard and Elizabeth when they lived in Pacoima, California.*

Bob Wesley also knew Howard Hill personally. Bob, Howard Fly, Paul Brunner, John Schulz, and Bob Wesley were a team participating in the 1978 National Bowhunt. The team, sponsored by John Schulz, won with American Longbow bows and Hill's shooting technique.

Image 112. Howard Fly, John Schulz, Paul Brunner, and Bob Wesley, 1978.

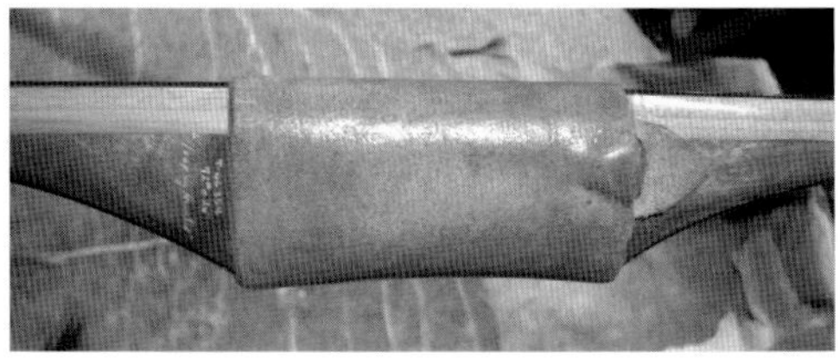

Image 113. Medicine Ram, by John Schulz for Paul Brunner.

Image 114. Master John Schulz, hitting 'em like Howard Hill.

References:
John Schulz, *Hitting 'em Like Howard Hill*
John Schulz, *Straight Shooting*
Bob Wesley, *Traditional Archery Adventures and Tips for Better Shooting*
Nate Steen, conversation regarding the Hill-style quiver.

Byron Ferguson

Byron Ferguson

Image 115. Byron Ferguson, Master of the Longbow.

The most popular trick shooter at present is Byron Ferguson. We can confidently say so. Just like Howard Hill, Byron makes a living out of his shows and products sold under his name. I assume he also has advertising contracts with archery and hunting manufacturers.

Byron was born on October 31, 1953, in Moulton, Alabama. At the age of twelve, he began working as a bricklayer's assistant to earn money to purchase his first recurve. Today he is a longbow archer. When he was a child, Byron was deeply impressed by veteran archer and fellow Alabaman, Howard Hill.

Byron shoots aluminum arrows with natural fletching. Making suitable and accurate wooden arrows for Ferguson's precision shots be too complicated. Also like Hill, Ferguson uses a back quiver. A back quiver allows smooth maneuvering, a great advantage when trick shooting, especially at moving targets. Ferguson does not use any sights or other gadgets.

One of Byron's famous and incredible tricks is the coin trick. An assistant, usually his wife Wanda, throws a dime into the air and Byron's blunt arrow hits it. Watch this trick in slow motion on Mr. Ferguson's video, *Become the Arrow*. Be sure to prepare some popcorn—most people watch the trick again and again. He once shot eight dimes in a row out of the air.

Image 116. Byron discussing arrows for a German TV program.

He does the same trick with aspirin tablets—another popcorn situation.

Another trick is the card trick, in which he splits a playing card in half from the side, where it is only as thick as a sheet of paper.

Byron Ferguson is obviously living Howard Hill's philosophy:

> *If you want to become a good archer then you should learn the bow and let your body become an extension of the bow. If you want to become a great archer, you should let your body become the arrow.*

Watch Ferguson shoot once and you will realize that he has become the arrow. He uses some kind of point of aim system and a style modeled after Howard Hill.

I would recommend Ferguson's book, *Become the Arrow,* to every traditional archer, and in particular, every novice. Byron describes his style, his method of aiming, his training, his equipment, and lots of other things worth knowing. It's a book you will read more than once.

In 2009, I edited the German language version of this book and it sells well here in Europe. Most German writers on shooting techniques refer to writings by Byron Ferguson and G. Fred Asbell as the basics.

At this point I would like to add the following. I often ask myself, from which method or role model are today's archery novices learning how to shoot. When I began shooting there was the FITA-style and its variants and then there were the "string-walkers," those who use the arrow point as a reference. Compound shooters don't need a shooting style. I didn't like either of these methods—it was not my idea of archery. Therefore, I obtained books and videos from the US. The English, whom I regarded as inventors of longbow shooting, shot their longbows FITA-style. That's why I stuck to the Americans, to Dr. Pope, Fred Bear, and Howard Hill. Various sources and friends that I came across during my quest for proper archery led me to the Hill-style. When I first saw a video of Hill depicting his shooting form, seemingly easy and effortless to learn, I knew immediately that that was how to shoot the bow.

I don't think that Hill's style is *the* one and only, but I believe that many novices would benefit from modeling their shooting style after a proven, functional method. Films by Byron Ferguson, G. Fred Asbell, John Schulz, Bob Wesley, and many others are excellent teaching aids for acquiring an effective and consistent style.

There is nothing esoteric about shooting the bow. There are no mysterious powers propelling the arrow towards its target. It is us, we are shooting; we, that is, includes the perfectly tuned equipment and you. Hitting the target depends on the quality of our practice and our style. Apart from some archers, who may have a heavenly, god-given talent, hitting the target is directly linked to the practice and training of a shooting form.

Everyone who knows me, has heard this sermon before, so please excuse the repetition.

Image 117. Bowman Erwin Leth, the author, and Byron Ferguson in Austria, 2010.

Image 118. Byron's equipment, a 66" longbow (70@ 28") Z-Bow made by his son Zachary and an Easton aluminium arrow tipped with a 220-grain, Muzzy Phantom broadhead.

Back to Byron Ferguson. The most difficult shot of his career, as Byron usually says, was a shot he performed on the live Japanese television show, *Super People.* He had to shoot an arrow through a diamond ring worth $17,000. The difficulty was that the first time he heard about the stunt was when the host of the show first introduced it to the live audience. But that really didn't matter to Byron. Even without any practice he made a perfect shot.

Byron was the first American archer since the legendary Howard Hill to tour Europe and demonstrate his tricks. After his performance at the National Game Fair, a hunting fair held on the grounds of the Chambord Castle in France, spectators named Byron, "King of the Show."

With his longbow, Byron has bagged more than 200 whitetail, plus wild hogs and black bears.

I am sure we will hear more from Mr. Ferguson. I would like to see this great archer perform live, but until then I will be content watching the films *Become the Arrow 1, Become the Arrow 2,* and Byron's other amazing movies. And I will have to accept the fact that I did not know about the Hill-style when I first learned how to shoot at age twelve.

In March 2010, I had the honor of meeting Byron Ferguson in Austria. He performed on stage in Granz, Styria, Austria. Since I was the editor of the German language edition of his great book, *Become the Arrow,* we were in contact before he arrived in Austria.

He and his wife Wanda are really great, humble folks. We shared a day with them as

Byron did some shooting for a German TV channel, trying to confirm stunt shots from Robin Hood movies. He executed all of these shots with grace and I could see that Byron is an exceptional shot with the longbow. He confirmed that all shots were doable.

One shot was to cut a gallows rope at 60 yards. Byron used his 70-pound Z-Bow, which his son Zachary made, and an Easton Legacy arrow fletched with five high profile feathers and a 220-grain Muzzy Phantom broadhead. The Master of the Longbow just raised the bow and let fly. He missed the rope, shooting about one inch on the right side. In elevation he had no problem shooting the middle of that approximately 60-inch rope.

With three shots he scratched the rope, so it unravelled. I was amazed. He was not able to cut that gallows rope from that distance, but cut it then from about 30 yards. When I went to the backstop, I found his arrows sticking within an 8-inch circle.

I'm looking forward to meeting Byron again in 2011 here in Austria. We plan to make a shooting school DVD for European longbow aficionados. He is a great name in worldwide archery, and I'm happy to know that Alabama bow wizard.

Image 119. The master explaining his "Become the Arrow" method after an amazing show.

References:
Byron Ferguson, *Become the Arrow*
T.J. Conrads, *Traditional Bowhunter Magazine*
Byron Ferguson's website (www.byronferguson.com) and one of his photo CDs.

Austrian Archery

Alois Zopf

In each country of the world there was a need for a special kind of man to rediscover the bow and arrow, which, since the invention of firearms, had almost been forgotten. In the US there were several archery pioneers, some of which you can find in this book. It is impossible to give an exhaustive list of everyone who patronized archery, but think of Pete Shepley, Gail Martin, Earl Hoyt, Jim Dougherty, Doug Easton, Chester Stevenson, Jay Massey, Glenn St. Charles, Robert Elmer, George L. Herter, J. A. Davies, Roy Hoff, and Harry Drake, just to name a few.

Image 121. Two European beauties, a Porsche 911 and a Zopf bow, designed after a Black Widow model.

We should not forget that behind many of these men there were women supporting all their archery follies, keeping their straying men on a long and obviously loose leash. But there were also numerous women who left a lasting impact on archery: Ann Marston, Myrtle Miller, M. E. Howell, Jean Lee Lombardo, Ann Weber Hoyt, Dorothy Cummings, Babe Bitzenberger, Lura R. Wilson, Florence Lillie, Ann Clark, Doreen Wilber, and Julia Body, again, just to name a few.

Image 122. A stylish Austrian archer.

In Western Europe, especially in the German-speaking countries, which don't have a long archery tradition to look back on like the English, there were only a few people dedicated to the bow and arrow and able to influence the archery scene. Alois Zopf of Bad Goisern, Austria, is one of them. It was an honor for me to speak with this father of European archery. Today, he is retired and has a house, which naturally has a bow workshop, in Hungary where he spends his time with his wife Elisabeth. We enjoyed a cup of tea with a dash of rum and Elisabeth, the perfect hostess, served a perfect alpine snack. Elisabeth Zopf is still involved in Alois' passion for the bow and arrow. For decades she has been making strings and arrows, always supporting her husband's ideas and fervor. And Alois is still making bows, but he has given his archery shop, Bogensport Zopf, in Bad Goisern (in Austria's Salzkammergut region) to his grandson. It is one of Austria's and Europe's oldest archery shops.

Image 123. The Zopf Archery shop in Bad Goisern, Austria.

Alois Zopf was born on February 24, 1933, in Bad Goisern, Austria. His mother ran a book and paper shop, his father was a mountain guide, skiing instructor, and sporting goods outfitter. Alois' grandfather had been the mountain guide for Elisabeth, Empress of Austria (the legendary "Sissi"). The imperial family spent a good deal of time in the beautiful Salzkammergut resort area, and there are many anecdotes about Emperor Franz Josef hunting chamois, deer, and mouflon sheep.

Image 124. Alois managed some very innovative archery events.

Alois was trained as a bookseller but also became a mountain guide, skiing instructor, and sporting goods outfitter. In 1956, Alois attended an event at the Schileiten Skiing School, where various summer sports were being presented. Mr. Walter Rauch of the Pohl sporting goods company in Vienna was introducing archery. Mr. Rauch was a charismatic man, presenting bows and arrows and other tackle. Alois bought some of his arrows and a wooden flatbow and from this day on he was smitten with archery. In nearby Bad Ischl he found a few friends sharing his passion, and at the local sports club an archery group was founded.

Image 125. Zopf at a ski-archery tournament.

Zopf took over his parents' book and sports shop in 1958. He began selling WINGS-bows, low-priced ash flatbows, and semi-recurves that he ordered from the Tinnefeld company.

A year later he imported Seefab steel bows and metal arrows from Sweden. Then, in 1960, he also offered Apollo steel bows from England.

In 1962, Zopf went to Tokyo, Japan, to see Mr. Onuma who was running a Kyudo archery shool, and for the first time Alois saw wooden composite bows made by Yamaha. These proper recurve bows were made of maple lams and fiberglass. This ushered in a new era in Austrian archery, as shooting was immediately improved with these new bows. Alois imported bamboo-laminated recurve bows made by the San-Ei Co. in Tokyo for archers at the front of Austrian archery, like Oswald Probst, Hartmut Wirt, Kurt Dworak, Hans Peter Ludwig, and Walter Rekirsch.

Alois told me that back then there was only little contact with the US. In 1962, Alois begins producing laminated hickory bows with the Kunze cabinetmaking company, which was run by an archer, too.

Image 126. Russian archer, Viktor Sidoruk, European Champion 1970, with a Zopf Super 8 model.

In 1963, Alois imported the FITA world champ, Frantisek Hadas, from Prague. Many of the imported Japanese bows were faulty, breaking at the tips—sometimes the whole limb broke. Frantisek Hadas, who turned out to be a genius technician, was able to repair many of these bows. Alois Zopf contacted the American company Easton and took over as their aluminium arrow representative.

In 1964, Zopf brought the US company Hoyt to Europe. He cooperated with other manufacturers as well, including Saunders, Damon Howatt, Ben Pearson, USAC, and Black Widow. Obviously, the US was regarded as a leader in the development and marketing of archery equipment.

In 1965, Zopf established his own bow workshop. He developed the Saturn I, a recurve bow sold as a youth tournament bow. The bow, which had a puristic aesthetic, turned out to be a best seller. Saturn bows from this production line are still in use today, according to Alois, who told me there is a rehabilitation center in Bad Häring that uses them.

The recurve bows that Alois produced had limbs made of solid great maple lams. The backings and facings were Gordon Bo-tuff glass, and for grip wood, Zopf usually used Bubinga.

In 1966, Doug Easton visited Alois Zopf in Bad Goisern. Zopf archery products were exhibited at all major sporting goods trade fairs. The Zopf line consisted of the following models: Diana, Merkur, Saturn I, and Saturn II.

In 1967, Zopf designed Saturn III and X7, the latter got its name when Alois' seventh child was born. I guess not all nights were dedicated to bow-making. Champion Anni Berner won the Euro Cup with a Zopf *X7*. In 1967, Hans Peter Ludwig shot Austria's first 1100-FITA star with a Saturn III bow.

When I visited the Zopfs, as it always happens among archers, we covered various topics, from technical details to archery history to the latest trends and gossip. Alois Zopf is one of those calm, modest experts. Actually, there are many who believe themselves to be experts, but Lois, as his friends call him, is truly impressive. I believe we can trust a man who initiated complete bow production and put all his energy into a rather exotic sport back then. He has left a lasting impact on the development of archery in Europe.

Image 127. World Champion, Frantisek Hadas.

Image 128. Alois Zopf, second from left, with friends.

Image 129. Alois Zopf, always promoting archery, formed the Austrian branch of FITA.

In 1968, Zopf introduced the Super 8 to the archery world. The handle was made of rosewood, or Bubinga, and the limbs were made of the tried and true great maple glass system.

Together with Franz Urbanek from Vienna, Alois developed a metal grip zone for a three-part recurve bow. Alois designed a prototype according to the needs of the FITA shooters and called the model Alu Magic. Zopf was the first worldwide to produce a metal handle for a three-part bow.

In 1970, the Russian Viktor Sidoruk won the European Championship in Hradec Králové, Czech Republic, with a Zopf Super 8 bow. Production of the Alu Magic began. Siegfried Ortman from Germany and the Robert Coginaux from Belgium won lots of tourneys with the Alu Magic. The Alu Magic and the Golden Eagle were the first takedown recurves made in the world. The Alu Magic is definitely more sophisticated. Two years later, Alois introduced a magnesium grip zone made by Hoyt. Earl Hoyt was quite the innovator. He invented the duo-stabilizing system with spider stabilizer and limbs that had a foamed core.

In 1971, Alois Zopf built a new workshop that was nearly 5,400 square feet. Until then, the Alu Magic handle had been made by sand casting, but with the extra space Alois could use a mold method. Back then, the mold alone cost 40,000 Deutschmark. Alois Zopf developed a special sight and a stabilizing system.

In 1972, the Zopf production facility had 20 employees. The Alu Magic handle, boasting a high-end varnish in various colors, is now made by pressure casting. Alois signed a sales contract for more than 1,000 Alu Magic bows in Osaka, Japan. Camiel Tytgat sold 300 Alu Magic bows per year. The Alu Magic became the FITA bow par excellence. Many champions shoot Zopf's sophisticated bows. Jim Easton visited Alois in Bad Goisern, Austria.

From 1973 to 1975, the Alu Magic sold well and production was in top gear. Elisabeth, Alois's wife, was making makes 10-15,000 bow strings per year.

For Crown Prince Reza Pahlavi, son of His Imperial Majesty the Shah Reza

Pahlavi, Alois made a miniature bowset on the occasion of the prince's sixth birthday. It included a beautiful arrow case emblazoned with the Royal Persian Crest, a red leather scabbard, and a beautifully decorated quiver and arm guard.

Image 130. Alois managed breathtaking, alpine archery events.

In 1976, however, there was a terrible downturn in business. Previously, all sales were in US dollars, so when the dollar was devaluated it severely affected Alois' bottom line. For example, in 1971 Zopf received 2,350 Austrian Schillings for 100 US dollars, but in 1976, it was down to 1,560 Schillings. Further production would result in serious losses. In 1977, Alois terminated production and turned the workshop into a sports shops. Responding to this new economic situation, Zopf imported renowned brands, including Hoyt, Bear, Yamaha, Greenhorn, Easton, PSE, Martin, Flex Fletch, Beman, Arizona, AGF, Bjorn Bengston, Merlin, and many other brands. With these products, too, Alois was the market leader in Austria. Every archer, FITA aficionado or traditional shooter, could purchase whatever he or she wanted at Alois' shop: Hoyt Gold Medalist bows, Western Standard bows, compounds by PSE, Bear Metric Magnum arrows, sights, and every imaginable type of tackle.

In 1988, Zopf again enlarged his program, optimizing his return by bundling up purchases and thereby reducing transportation expenses.

Over the years, Alois' wife Elisabeth has made thousands of bowstrings and all kinds of arrows. Now, Elisabeth has taken over the book and paper shop, their son Thomas Zopf runs the sports shops, and Alois concentrates on his bows. On the side Alois runs an Adventure Center and a skiing school.

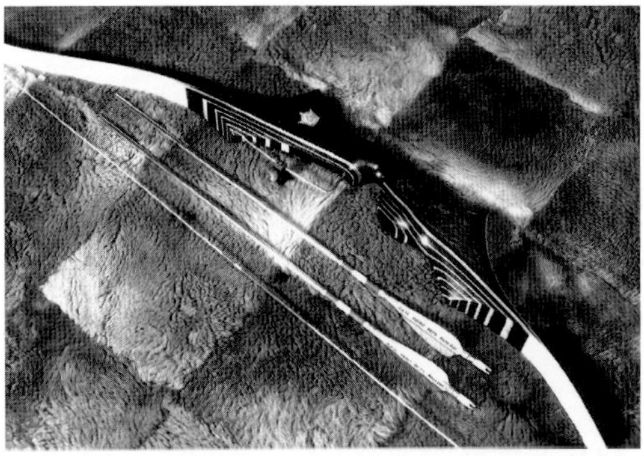

Image 131 and 132. The archery set for the Prince of Persia's sixth birthday.

I have really enjoyed my conversations with Alois Zopf in preparation for this book. He knows everything there is to know about bows and the archery scene. He regrets that there are hardly any Austrian or German FITA successes worldwide. The 3D scene, with its sometimes slack tourneys and poor financial assistance, could be a reason.

But Lois does not feel disgruntled; as he has always done in his archery life, he recognizes and appreciates that the bow and arrow are currently enjoying a renaissance. Presumably, there have never been more bowmen and bowhunters than today. We all agree that the massive influx from the re-enactment scene, from the lines of attention-seekers, the *Lord of the Rings* bow-buyers is a less pleasant factor. People who only know these types of bowmen might get the impression that archers are from a different planet. But then again, that's true; even though we don't disguise ourselves, archers are a bit different compared to most people.

Zopf organized a unique 3D tournament in the massive cave in the Dachstein mountain. He organized tournaments in extremely mountainous areas and archers had to be secured with ropes. Zopf ski-archery competitions were broadcast on German TV.

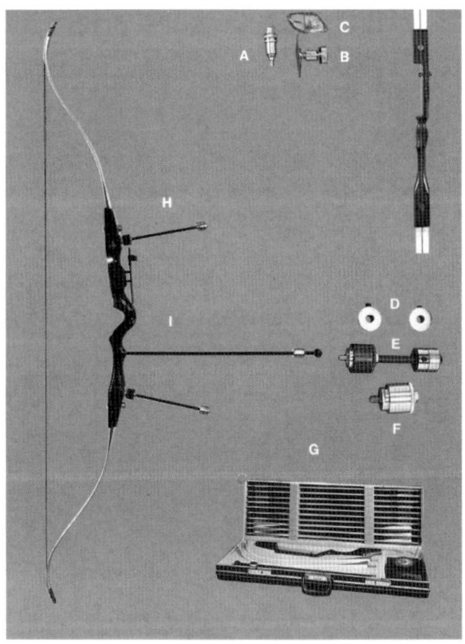

Image 133. Alu Magic

Image 134. Fritz Sieler, Vienna, 1969 at one of Lois' Ski-Archery Events.

I got to know Alois Zopf when he personally delivered 3D targets to our longbow archers club. He had always been modest, and he should therefore not be forgotten. Through Alois I got to know a second important man at the front of Austrian archery—Michael Sarnitz.

Image 135. Alois Zopf and the author, checking out recurve bows.

Michael Sarnitz

Michael Sarnitz

Image 136. Michael Sarnitz crossing the Kalahari desert.

When he was a student, Sarnitz bought his first bow, a Saturn, at Zopf's shop. Since then, they have developed a friendship. It's always the same—names that matter are never mentioned, if we think of all those club officials supporting, organizing, and structuring archery for all our benefit, who knows there names? They aren't mentioned in any book.

By the late 1980s, early 1990s, I was gripped by archery fever. Hunting stores and outfitters offered archery tackle and Bear bows. They usually had Bear Archery catalogs. I still remember the German Robin Sport catalog, and Jennings Archery, which belonged to Bear Archery at that time. I dug up a catalog from somewhere: SACO was the name of the Austrian company. It was a beautiful catalog with informative stories, great pictures, and photos. Of course, at that time, the compound bow was the future and there were lots of models designed for hunting purposes and target bows in various designs and colors. Some photos showed a lean, dark-haired man in adventurous positions and outfits in exotic countries. It was Mike Sarnitz. One day I acquired a training folder that Mike Sarnitz, the European representative par excellence, gave to Bear and SACO Archery shops. A complete and sophisticated program, providing technical know-how, good customer service, and clear guidelines for archery. Thinking of the countless outfitters that have emerged in Germany and Austria in recent years, I believe some of them could do with such a training guide. Competence results in loyal clients; that's a timeless law.

Image 137. Mike Sarnitz and Papa Bear.

SACO products were made by Bear Archery and other partners, but sold under the label SACO. On the bows it said: "Designed by Mike Sarnitz." I also liked that lots of archery equipment was in this catalog. On the back cover there were very good instructions on how to shoot the bow. Then, one day, I stopped hearing about SACO. During archery shots, I often saw three-piece recurve bows, the SACO Hunter model. I used to have one, too; it was of solid design, poisonous, and a workhorse. I shot it with bronze-colored Bear Metric Magnum arrows with natural fletching, and from the shelf. Generally, there was a trend towards rubber arrow rests. When I converted to the longbow faith, I gave the bow away. In 2009, I remembered Mike Sarnitz, wondering whether there were Austrian archery pioneers I could present in the US edition of this book. I remembered two men: Alois Zopf and Mike Sarnitz. I knew Alois Zopf and we had agreed to meet for an interview. Alois Zopf gave me Mike's phone number. I explained to him what I wanted to do—he liked the idea and we met at Mike's studio in Vienna. He had been thumbing through *Legends in Archery*. Mike was very professional and we began work immediately. Prior to the meeting, he had e-mailed a list of questions written by a renowned compound manufacturer, asking me to use them when interviewing Mike. After the interview we continued to talk about archery. Mike was friendly and impressed me. He is like a gentleman, a cosmopolitan. He has driven a Land

Rover through Africa and been hunting with Fred Bear—he was an adventurer with a passion for the bow and arrow. But he is also a successful, modern businessman. And, of course, always up-to-date with the archery world. Thinking in different dimensions, he knows how many archers there are in South America or Indonesia, and where future markets are found. At the same time, he knows everything about archery heritage worldwide.

For a second, my longbow archer's heart skipped a beat when I realized that I was doing an interview for a compound bow company. During the interview I learned that you should not categorize bowmen. The longbow archer's arrogance fell off me like droppings from an old horse when Mike gave me a detailed introduction to bow and arrow equipment from all over the world. When I noticed a large poster of Prince Valiant, Mike explained that he had always been a big fan. When I told him that I had the complete hardback edition, he answered, "Well, that makes things clear; we'll get along well."

Image 138. Mike Sarnitz and the author.

During the interview, which provided me with answers and new ideas, Mike was always impressive, easygoing, and totally professional. His assistant videotaped the exchange. The video was shown at the Archery Trade Association (ATA Trade Show in Columbus, Ohio, in 2010.

After the interview we were talking about the archery scene, new trends, and markets, as well as books on Fred Bear and Peter Shepley and Mike's journeys. I didn't ask him dry, biographical questions—chatting idly would be a better use of our time. He would forward his biography to me. It was an interesting evening. Mike regards the bow as something global and ancient—an eternal topic among archery aficionados, whether they live in Congo or Greenland, shoot a compound or a pygmy bow. All archers have the same problems and feel the same joy when shooting the bow, or philosophizing about archery.

Image 139. Mike Sarnitz and a Bushman chatting about poisoned broadheads.

Mike Sarnitz was born on August 2, 1950, in Vienna, Austria. After World War II, his parents Franz and Monika Sarnitz founded a distribution company dealing mainly in hunting and shooting products, such as rifles, shotguns, optical goods, and hunting accessories. While Mike's two sisters were more into arts, little Mike sneaked into the warehouse at any given opportunity. The employees did not dare send the little boy back to the house, as Franz Sarnitz led the company in a rather authoritarian style. This enabled the boy to handle and experience the various products he found on the shelves: airguns, rifles, knives, darts, etc. Truly, a little boy's paradise.

Mike's favorite literature was Prince Valliant by the famous artist Hal Foster. The bow and arrow were featured prominently in these beautiful early comic strips. For this reason, Mike always looked for bows, unfortunately not part of their program, in the warehouse. Mike, therefore, built his own stickbow in the garden.

In 1965, the martial art of karate was introduced to Austria and Mike attended an introductory course that helped him get through the challenges of adolescence. At the same time, his father Franz, who was on the National Trap-Shooting Team, competed in the 1960 Olympic Games in Rome. Mike's parents discovered that their son was not particularly talented at school. After he failed out of high school three times, they decided to send him to work in an ammunition factory in Birmingham, England. There, Mike earned his first money and was very happy to be away from "theoretical education."

Mike also became a member of the National Karate Team (Karate literally means "empty hands") and won the Austrian National Championships in 1969, the very same year his father became National Trap-Shooting Champion. Franz was touched when he and his son were honored at Town Hall by the mayor of Vienna, who announced that both had won the Nationals in their respective sports—the father with a weapon and the son without.

After his time in England, he came home only once or twice a year, Mike spent eleven years overseas to learn new languages and explore new marketing strategies at distribution companies in various countries. This was followed by Japan, the United States, and South Africa.

In 1970, Mike was team captain of the National Karate Team at the First Karate World Championships in Tokyo. Even though he had only made little stickbows as a boy, his interest in the bow and arrow continued despite a lack of instruction and literature on the sport. The World Championships in Tokyo were a turning point for him. This is where he first saw Japanese archery, called Kyudo ("the way of the bow"), and the Art of Yabusame (archery on horseback).

When Mike returned to Europe, he came across the Fred Bear catalog, distributed at this time by Winchester. The appearance of this catalog, with its wonderful motifs, nature and products combined, created so much enthusiasm in the young man, that he returned to the United States and applied to be a trainee at the Fred Bear Factory. After only a short time, the young fellow developed a close relationship with Fred Bear, the pioneer of archery. Fred Bear had no successor or son, and this, apart from commercial considerations, could have been the reason for selling the company. Fred stayed on as a promoter of the company and still designed recurve bows, while the development of compound bows caused a dramatic change in the archery industry. At this time, Tom Jennings, father of the modern compound bow, possessed various patents and became the spearhead of the compound bow market. Bear Archery picked up the compound bow, whose popularity was growing at a healthy pace, leaving the recurve bow far behind.

Image 140. Mike practicing horseback archery in the '80s—he looked like a gentleman, not like a Hun.

Image 141. Because of the lack of water, Mike had to switch from horse to camel while traveling through the Kalahari.

While Mike was staying in South Africa, working at a distribution company in Durban, every year he returned to the Bear factory, which moved from Michigan to Florida, to receive updates on the latest developments.

After South Africa, Mike earned enough money to buy a used Land Rover. He drove up to Europe through Africa in one year and seventeen days. During this trip, Bear bows were always with him, as firearms were totally prohibited throughout Africa. Mike picked up hunting techniques from his encounters with the Bushmen in the Kalahari and the Pygmies in the Congo basin.

In 1977, Mike arrived back in Vienna and had to take over the company as president because his father had a heart attack. The company specialized in exclusive representations and Bear Archery products were distributed on an exclusive basis within Austria. With a lot of enthusiasm, Mike started seminars for retailers, but Bear Archery was wondering why one of the smallest countries purchased proportionately more product than others. They invited Mike to the US for further talks regarding distribution. In 1981, Mike and Charles T. Smith, president of Bear Archery, signed a contract for all of Europe on an exclusive basis. Now, container shipments full of archery tackle went over the Atlantic, which had an impact on the international archery market.

Image 142. Different technologies, same spirit.

In 1984, Dr. Jim Shubert, and some of Mike's other very enthusiastic friends, founded the World Bowhunting Association. During his marketing trips throughout the world, Mike approached the various authorities in the different countries to explain and demonstrate the ethical aspects and the most efficient equipment for hunting game. Although this process is still developing, quite a number of countries have legalized bowhunting as an ethical hunting form, and in 1986, Mike received the Hall of Honor Award from SCI for the promotion of archery worldwide. A couple of years before, in 1983, Fred Bear had been the first to receive this award. Mike was especially honored to receive this award after Fred Bear. Most unfortunately, Fred died the very same year. Mike had accompanied his fatherly friend to various shows and tournaments during the last few years of Fred's life, helping him carry a machine that supported Fred's breathing. Mike was saddened by his loss.

From 1987 till 1992, Mike's responsibility widened, as his responsibilities became global, with the exception of the US and Canada. Apart from the marketing challenges, he timed his trips in such a way that after visiting customers he could change into his outdoor outfit and escape civilization to tribes that were still bowhunting. In the majority of the cases, Mike was lucky to encounter the last hunters with very simple gear, explore their ability to survive in the wilderness, and learn the skills of approaching game. His visits to tribes in Asia, South America, and Africa (a book is in the works) helped him understand the true values of life. In 1992, Mike's father died and he sold his shares of the company to become an independent agent for various archery manufacturers worldwide.

Image 143. Bowfishing with the Yagua Indians in the Itaqui River, Colombia.

Of course, I was impressed by Mike's direct link to Fred Bear, whom I have always admired; there is no bowman or outdoorsman who wouldn't be. Fred, with his open personality and the way he dealt with people, never failed to impress anyone with a heart for the wilderness and a life outdoors.

Mike told me a typical Fred Bear story:

Late summer 1978, I joined Bear Archery as trainee at their plant which had just been transferred from Michigan to the beautiful Southern state Florida. For me, it was like heaven, due to the fact that I had never seen a factory combining manufacturing processes, a museum, and a wonderful archery course around the factory, including a fresh water pond. Fred knew me as a skeptical rifle hunter who was not aware of the efficiency of the bow and arrow for harvesting game. I personally could just not imagine it, being brought up in a very conservative and traditional way in regard to hunting. After work, Fred sneaked into my office, both hands in his pockets and said, "Mike, do you have a minute, I'd like to show you my museum." I was more than thrilled that the big guy himself wanted to give me a tour of his own museum. After all the workers had left, Fred and myself went up to the first floor, walking along a wonderfully decorated hallway, where I could not only see full and head-mounted trophies, but also on the other side of the hallway, the whole manufacturing machinery through a big show-window enabling the general spectator to see both the artifacts of the museum, mounted animals, and bows and arrows of primitive tribes, and on the other side, the whole factory with all the production. I was rather speechless, which Fred realized and therefore put his arm around me, strolling with me through the museum and telling me stories which connected him with the appropriate animal. He sensed in my behavior, that I still could not imagine that you have to approach game from a very close distance, contrary to rifle hunting; at the end of this late evening he asked, "Would you like to join me over the weekend to hunt some whitetail bucks?" I murmured a shy, "I would love to do so." So, Fred picked me up on Friday after work and we arrived, after a four-hour drive, at a specific hunting ground. The log cabin that we slept in, would have been, for every young hunter, the absolute, ultimate, a dream come true, even without or before successfully hunting anything. Over the next few days, it seemed to be pretty difficult to locate the tracks of whitetail bucks in the area, so after two or three hours of tracking and scouting we went back to the log cabin. However, this time was used to talk about draw weights, spine of the arrow, and broadheads. I thought to myself, this particular weekend would be more a theoretical one, and being an impatient young guy, I was a bit disappointed that we had not even seen a single animal. We did some practice in the log cabin, although Fred would not allow me yet to use the bow—but that would be the deal, he had already stated that prior to our hunting excursion. Although I did already have some good grouping, it´s a completely different story to shoot at a target versus hunting an animal. At 4 p.m. on Sunday, we went out again and Fred put me in a ground blind while he was in a tree stand approximately five meters above the ground. We both overlooked the forest opening and had eye contact. After so many unsuccessful excursions, I was a bit frustrated and did a little bit of drawing in my diary, as my assumption was that nothing would show up. At the very same moment, four does and three male whitetails came out to the opening and started feeding. I was at a distance of approximately 20 meters, while Fred's tree stand, at his particular angle, must have been around 16 meters. They were feeding for a couple of minutes and the wind blew in perfect direction towards us. It was a wonderful sight, especially the big whitetail buck that did not feed at first, but was a bit cautious before it also started feeding. Suddenly I heard the twang of Fred's string and all the animals went off, highly disturbed. I heard and actually saw an arrow falling to the ground as the opening was covered with little stones. My immediate reaction was, "Oh my god, he missed", and I was convinced that my prejudice and skepticism towards this hunting form were justified. The hunt was over and I put on a friendly smile, starting to say to Fred, "Missing is part of hunting". However, my smile immediately froze, when I saw that exactly the same big whitetail buck appeared again on the scene, trying to feed, but after a few seconds it went down on its hind legs, tried to stand up again and fell to the ground. I just could not figure out what was happening, the arrow away from the harvested buck, Fred on the tree stand and me in the ground blind. A few seconds of silence passed, and then I saw a big grin on Fred's face, with his thumb pointing up. He climbed down and I congratulated him in a very puzzled and astonished way. What had happened? The arrow from his 65-pound recurve Kodiak bow had gone right through the lung area, with the animal disappearing for probably 15 seconds and then returning to the feeding area. After having realized this incredible experience and how ethically and efficient this particular hunting gear was, I introduced Fred to our traditional way of congratulating the successful hunter, breaking two twigs, with Fred asking me, "What the hell are you doing?" I replied, "Two hunting cultures are now coming together and I, as a European, take this twig, put it into the mouth of the animal, honoring this wonderful creature, with the second twig put onto the blade of my hunting knife, handing it over to Fred, who took it after shaking hands, putting it on his Borsalino hat. He smiled and said, "I like that, I will introduce this amongst our hunters, but there will not be many twigs left in the future. Great stuff!" I was rather quiet on our way back home and something in my whole attitude changed. Fred just glanced at me, after a couple of hours of driving, sensing that there were a lot of things going through my head. Then he broke the silence and said, "When you get back home and you speak about bowhunting, never try to discriminate rifle hunters; but on the contrary, be patient and let them be part of our beautiful hunting form. Let them hunt with both: bow and rifle."

Image 144. Mike and Fred Bear with Fred's famous mounted Bear.

Mike's story confirmed my picture of Fred Bear. He was a decent man, a man with a passion for the bow and arrow, and a man who really understood people. Mike Sarnitz is a very charismatic man, too. Apart from making business trips all over the world, he is currently preparing a book which contains some of the following adventures:

- Hunting with the Bushmen in the Kalahari, Namibia
- Trans-Africa expedition with the Bear Recurve Supermagnum from Cape Town to Vienna
- Hunting with the Pygmies in the Congo Basin
- Journey to the Yagua Indians in a raft on the Amazon
- Leopard, the cattle killer in southern Sudan
- Encounter with the last hunters of Borneo: the Penang
- Survival with bow and arrow in the Yukon Territory
- Tranquilizing endangered species with the bow in South Africa
- The Akkahs of Burma—the last female bowhunters
- Expedition to the last Negritos in the Andamans

Image 145. Mike with an exceptional waterbuck.

The working title of the book is *Ancient Hunters of Today*. Mike has hunted with numerous original bowhunters in Asia, South America, Africa, and Oceania. His book is based on these experiences, documented with numerous photographs.

This, my brothers-in-arms, this native, original form of bowhunting is disappearing. It is our task to maintain and preserve bowhunting, our collective heritage. It should be possible for our descendants to experience this incredible feeling of hunting with the bow: nocking a broadhead, carefully treading our way, cautiously maneuvering through the wood, trailing fresh tracks, and catching a first glimpse of the game. Like the boxer in the boxing ring, the bowhunter is on his own, solely depending on his intuition, his skills.

What would life be without adventures, without those evenings around the campfire telling the true stories of the hunt with a good slug of whisky and a few good books?

References:
Conversations with *Michael Sarnitz* and *Alois Zopf*

Austrian Bowhunters

Image 146. Adi Maurer, Karl Hofmeister, Theo Schett, Gery Moser, Joerg Painsipp, and Richard Mayr, after a successful hunt in Quebec, Canada.

Image 147. Martin Huber, Tyrol, with a nice impala in South Africa.

Image 148. Karl Hofmeister, Styria, with his famous companion Rigo and a roe buck in Hungary.

Image 149. Theo Schett, Salzburg, and the author with a mouflon sheep in Hungary.

Image 150. Fred Schlögl, Burgenland, with a nice pair of carps.

Image 151. Heinz Stroher, Styria, with a heavy black bear in British Columbia, Canada.

Image 152. Joerg Painsipp, Styria, with a good tusker in Queensland, Australia.

Image 153. Theo Schett, with a cinnamon bear in Idaho, USA.

Image 154. Heinz Steiner, Salzburg, with an exceptional axis bull in Australia.

Image 155. Karl Hofmeister and Heinz Steiner with a roe buck in Hungary.

Image 156. Martin Huber with an exceptional waterbuck, South Africa.

Image 157. Theo Schett and Karl Hofmeister with a caribou in Canada.

Image 158. Fritz Massinger, Tyrol, with a nice warthog in Namibia.

Image 159. The author with a wild boar in Hungary.

Image 160.Karl Hofmeister with an impala in South Africa.

Image 161. Fritz Massinger with an impala in Namibia.

Image 162. The author with a boar in Hungary.

Image 163. The author, Theo Schett, and Karl Hofmeister celebrating Theo's African trophies.

Image 164. The author with a small carp.

Image 165. Karl Hofmeister harpooned a much smaller one.

Image 166. Theo Schett chasing a black bear in Idaho, USA.

Robin Hood and the End

Robin Hood and the End

There are many stories, films, and plays about Robin Hood. I thought a book about legendary bowmen that did not mention Robin Hood would not be worth reading. I had to write about him, believing that part of his spirit can be found in every archer.

A good book about him is *Robin Hood* by James C. Holt. It analyzes legends, ballads, and the historical background surrounding the archer in Lincoln green clothes. Reading that book, I broadened my previously incomplete knowledge of Robin Hood and his merry men.

Robert Fitz-Ooth, Robertus Hodus, or Robert Hode is said to have lived from 1160 until 1247. He was the leader of a group of benevolent outlaws living in Sherwood Forest. There are no clear records from Robin Hood's time, but in 1420, in his *Chronicle of Scotland* (*Orygynale Cronykil*), Andrew de Wyntoun dated Robin and Little John's adventures to a period of time between 1283 and 1285.

Presumably, the legend of Robin Hood and Richard the Lionheart were linked by historian John Major in his *History of Great Britain*, in 1521, declaring that Robin lived around 1193-94, when Richard the Lionheart was imprisoned after his crusade in Austria. Later on, other hints and allusions from various sources were included in the legend. One day, the name Locksley popped up and the Barnsdale area and the Kirklee Priory were added to the story.

In the seventeenth century, Thomas Gale described a headstone bearing the following inscription:

> *Here underneath this little stone,*
> *lies Robert, Earl of Huntington.*
> *No archer was as he so good,*
> *and people called him Robin Hood.*
> *Such outlaws as he and his men,*
> *will England never see again.*

According to James C. Holt, Maid Marian first appeared between 1450 and 1500 and Little John entered the legend around 1432. Friar Tuck was previously mentioned by Robert Stafford in 1417. And I could not find out when Will Scarlet, Allin-a-Dale and Much, the Miller's Son became members of the Hood-gang.

In Sir Walter Scott's *Ivanhoe*, the Robin Hood character Locksley plays an important role. Scott narrates the conflict between the Anglo-Saxons and Normans.

Over the years, other adventures and escapades entered the Robin Hood tales, even those attributed to other "heroes." Some people believe he was a woodland sprite from Old English mythology, a pixie, or the Green Man. Some sources point to the Celtic god Belenus. I believe that there is at least some truth in all those ballads, stories, or tales that mention him.

Numerous films have been made about Robin Hood, but few are as picturesque, romantic, and true to the legend as the 1938 Warner Brothers film, *The Adventures of Robin Hood,* with Errol Flynn playing the lead role and Olivia de Havilland as Maid Marian. Howard Hill was the Captain of Archers, responsible for all archery stunts.

Image 167. Howard Hill, Captain of Archers, and Errol Fynn, 1938, Warner Bros.

Another favorite of mine is the 1976 film, *Robin and Marian,* with Sean Connery as old Robin and Audrey Hepburn as wonderful Marian.

It does not matter if Robin Hood and his merry men, living in Sherwood Forest, really existed; but it is an established fact that even in modern times, his adventures are still known. Robin Hood's moral values—justice, bravery, loyalty, friendship, living in harmony with nature, and the love of freedom—are timeless.

If, one day, the existence of Robin Hood is really proven, I will look at my longbow, smile, and be happy. I will be happy for being right. I will say I have always known it and call my friends drawing forth my cellular bugle, "Let's gather at the oak…no, only English longbows and Lincoln green tights…no, maids only wearing long dresses...yes, we will bring a wooden cask of cool beer, and earthen mugs…. no, we will eat the king's venison…Yes, I still have a nice bit of fawn venison from August…"

Image 168. Robin Hood with his bugle horn.

You gentlemen and yeoman good,
come in and drink with Robin Hood;
If Robin Hood be not at home,
come in and drink with Little John.

Image 169. A merry man with English longbow.

Bibliography

Ahlefeldt, L. and Bille, G., *Impala*, 1937, Gyldendal

Anderson, Fred, *The Traditional Way: The Mystique and Heritage of Archery*, 1997, TOX Press

Asbell, G. Fred, *Stalking & Still-Hunting*, 1997, Hunter Image Prod.

Bear, Fred, *Fred Bear's Field Notes: The Adventures of Fred Bear*, 1976, The Fred Bear Sports Club Press

Bear, Fred, *The Archers Bible*, 1980, Doubleday & Company, Inc.

Bertalan, Dan, *Traditional Bowyers of America*, 1989, Envisage Unlimited Press

Burke, Edmund H., *Archery Handbook*, 1954, Arco Publishing Company Inc.

Capstick, Peter H., *The Last Ivory Hunter: The Saga of Wally Johnson*, 1988, St. Martin's Press

Carson, Don, *Early Adventures with Howard Hill*, 2004, Raptor Publishing, Inc.

Coe, Cliff, *44 Years Behind the Bow*, 1990, Montgomery County Tribune

Comstock, Paul, *Hit The Mark!*, 1992, Paul Comstock

Comstock, Paul, *The Bent Stick*, 1988, Paul Comstock

Conrads, T. J., *The Traditional Bowhunters Handbook*, 2003, TBM, Inc.

Davis, J. E., *Ye Sylvan Archer*, 1927-1943, NFAA

Duff, James, *Bows and Arrows*, 1927, Simon Archery Foundation

Duguid, Julian, *Green Hell*, 1931, Jonathan Cape Ltd.

Duguid, Julian, *Tiger Man*, 1932, Victor Gollancz Ltd.

Ehlebracht, Peter, *Heia Safari*, 1986, Ullstein Verlag GmbH

Ekin, Craig, *Howard Hill: The Man and the Legend*, 1982, Charger Productions, Inc.

Ferguson, Byron, *Become the Arrow*, 1994, Target Communications Corp.

Gillelan, G. Howard, *Complete Book of the Bow and Arrow*, 1971, Stackpole Books

Green, Roger Lancelyn, *The Adventures of Robin Hood*, 2001, The Folio Society, London

Hansard, George Agar, *The Book of Archery*, 1840, Longmans

Hardy, Robert, *Longbow: A Social and Military History*, 1976, Patrick Stephens Limited

Heath, E. G., *The Grey Goose Wing*, 1971, New York Graphic Society

Hemingway, Ernest, *Die Wahrheit im Morgenlicht*, 1999, Rowohlt

Higham, Charles, *Errol Flynn: The Untold Story*, 1980, Doubleday & Company, Inc.

Hill, Howard, *Hunting the Hard Way*, 1953, Willcox and Follett Co.

Hill, Howard, *Wild Adventure*, 1954, The Telegraph Press

Holt, James C., *Robin Hood*, 1991, Econ Verlag GmbH

Hougham, Paul C., *The Encyclopedia of Archery*, 1958, A. S. Barnes & Company

Hunt & Metz, *The Flatbow*, The Bruce Publishing Company

Kroll, Charles, *Fred Bear: Biography of an Outdoorsman*, 1988, The Fred Bear Sports Club Press

Lambert, Arther, W., *Modern Archery*, 1929, A. S. Barnes & Company

Lattimer, Dick, *I Remember Papa Bear*, 2005, ihunt! Communications

Massey, Jay, *The Book of Primitive Archery*, 1990, Bear Paw Publications

Massey, Jay, *The Bowyer's Craft*, 1987, Bear Paw Publications

Munger, Robert S., *Trailing a Bear*, 1995, The Munger Foundation

Negley, William, *Archer in Africa*, 1989, Amwell Press

Ortega y Gasset, José, *Meditations on Hunting*, 1972, Charles Scribner's Sons

Paluszeski, Alana, *Shooting Star*, 2007, Momentum Books, LLC

Pope, Saxton, *A Study of Bows and Arrows*, 1923, University of California Press

Pope, Saxton, *Hunting with the Bow and Arrow*, 1947, Popular Library

Pope, Saxton, *The Adventurous Bowmen*, 1926, G. P. Putnam's Sons

Pope, Saxton, *The Medical History of Ishi*, 1920, University of California Press

Pope, Saxton, *Yahi Archery*, 1918, University of California Press

Putnam, David Binney, *David Goes to Greenland*, 1926, G. P. Putnam's Sons

Schroeter, Willy, *Die Jagd- und Kriegswaffen der Indianer Nordamerikas*, 1991, Verlag für Amerikanistik

Schulz, John, *Hitting 'em Like Howard Hill*, 1975, John Schulz

Schulz, John, *Straight Shooting*, 2002, John Schulz

Schuyler, Keith C., *Archery, From Golds to Big Game*, 1970, Castle Books

Schuyler, Louis, *The Complete Archery Book*, 1957, Arco Publishing Company, Inc.

Shane, Adolph, *Archery Tackle*, 1990, Bois d' Arc Press

Siemel, Sasha, *Tigrero!*, 1953, Prentice-Hall Inc.

Swinehart, Bob, *In Africa*, 1967, The Boyertown Publishing Co.

Swinehart, Bob, *Sagittarius*, 1970, The Gallant Publishing Company

Thompson, Maurice, *The Witchery of Archery*, 1981, Sylvan Toxophilite Co.

Wensel, Gene, *The Best of Traditional Bowhunter*, 2005, Woodsman Publishing

Wesley, Bob, *Traditional Archery Adventures*, Universal Printing & Publishing

White, Steward Edward, *Lions in the Path*, 1926, Doubleday, Page & Company

Chapter Display Images

Chapter 1: Maurice Thompson, *The Witchery of Archery*
Chapter 2: Saxton Pope, *Yahi Archery*
Chapter 3: E. G. Heath, *The Grey Goose Wing*
Chapter 4: T. J. Conrads, *The Traditional Bowhunters Handbook*
Chapter 5: Saxton Pope, *Adventurous Bowmen*
Chapter 6: Saxtin Pope, *Hunting with the Bow and Arrow*
Chapter 7: Craig Ekin, Howard Hill: *The Man and the Legend*
Chapter 8: Fred Anderson, *The Traditional Way: The Mystique and Heritage of Archery*
Chapter 9: Author
Chapter 10: *Instinctive Archer Magazine*, Summer/Fall 1995
Chapter 11: Sasha Siemel, *Tigrero!*
Chapter 12: Charles Kroll, *Fred Bear*
Chapter 13: Fred Anderson, *The Traditional Way: The Mystique and Heritage of Archery*
Chapter 14: John Schulz, *Straight Shooting*
Chapter 15: William Negley, *Archer in Africa*
Chapter 16: Bob Swinehart, *Sagittarius*
Chapter 17: Author
Chapter 18: Ibid.
Chapter 19: Author
Chapter 20: Alois Zopf
Chapter 21: Michael Sarnitz
Chapter 22: Author
Chapter 23: Fred Anderson, *The Traditional Way: The Mystique and Heritage of Archery*

Photography Credits

Image 1. Author
Image 2. Saxton Pope
Image 3. Maurice Thompson
Image 4. Maurice Thompson, *The Witchery of Archery*, Sylvan Toxophilite Co, page 244
Image 5. Saxton Pope
Image 6. Ibid.
Image 7. E. G. Heath, *The Grey Goose Wing*, page 184
Image 8. T. J. Conrads, *The Traditional Bowhunters Handbook*, page 19
Image 9. Saxton Pope
Image 10. Ibid.
Image 11. Author
Image 12. Saxton Pope, *The Adventurous Bowmen*, page 44
Image 13. Wade Phillips, *Broadheads 1871-1971*
Image 14. Fred Anderson, *The Traditional Way: The Mystique and Heritage of Archery*, page 167
Image 15. David Putnam
Image 16. Saxton Pope
Image 17. Illustrations from *Hunting with the Bow and Arrow*
Image 18. T. J. Conrads, TBM
Image 19. *Instinctive Archer Magazine*, Summer/Fall 1996, page 43, Photo by Dave Rauschenberg
Image 20. Saxton Pope, *A Study of Bows and Arrows*, 1923, page 53
Image 21. Howard Hill, *Wild Adventure*, 1954, The Stackpole Company, page 87
Image 22. T. J. Conrads, *The Traditional Bowhunters Handbook*, 2003, TBM, Inc.
Image 23. Saxton Pope, *The Adventurous Bowmen*, Wolfe Publishing Company 1991
Image 24. Ibid., page 55
Image 25. Ibid.
Image 26. Craig Ekin, *Howard Hill: The Man and the Legend*, Charger Productions, Inc. 1982, page 47
Image 27. Fred Anderson, *The Traditional Way: The Mystique and Heritage of Archery*, 1997, Tox Press, Fred Anderson, page 188
Image 28. Ibid., page 52
Image 29. Ibid., page 188
Image 30. Phot by Ron LaClair
Image 31. Fred Anderson, *The Traditional Way: The Mystique and Heritage of Archery*, page 80
Image 32. Author
Image 33. Howard Hill, *Archery Adventures*, 1955, Trend Book, page 37, page 125
Image 34. Author
Image 35. Ibid.
Image 36. Fred Anderson, *The Traditional Way: The Mystique and Heritage of Archery*, 1997, Tox Press, Fred Anderson, page 208
Image 37. Ken Brown, *Bowfishing*, Ken Brown Publications, 1980, page 59
Image 38. T. J. Conrads, *The Traditional Bowhunters Handbook*, 2003, TBM, Inc.
Image 39. Ibid.
Image 40. Author
Image 41. Ibid.
Image 42. Bill Negley, *Archer in Africa*, Amwell Press 1989, page 35
Image 43. Author
Image 44. Craig Ekin, *Howard Hill: The Man and the Legend*, Charger Productions, Inc. 1982, page 154
Image 45. Sasha Siemel, *Tigrero!*, Prentice-Hall, 1953, page 124
Image 46. Ted Fry, Oregon
Image 47. Sasha Siemel, *Tigrero!*, Prentice-Hall, 1953
Image 48. Author
Image 49. Columbia Pictures, *Jungle Menace*, 1937

Image 50. Sasha Siemel, *Tigrero!*, Prentice-Hall, 1953
Image 51. Author
Image 52. Charles Kroll, *Fred Bear*, 1988, page 268
Image 53. Ibid., page 53
Image 54. Ibid., page 43
Image 55. Ibid., page 86
Image 56. Ibid., page 57
Image 57. Dick Lattimer, *I Remember Papa Bear*, 2005, page 49
Image 58. Charles Kroll, *Fred Bear*, 1988, page 92
Image 59. Dick Lattimer, *I Remember Papa Bear*, 2005
Image 60. Charles Kroll, *Fred Bear*, 1988, page 64
Image 61. Author
Image 62. Charles Kroll, *Fred Bear*, 1988, page 292
Image 63. Ibid., page 235
Image 64. Ibid., page 253
Image 65. Bear Archery Catalog
Image 66. Fred Bear, *The Archer's Bible*, 1968, page 127
Image 67. Dick Lattimer, *I Remember Papa Bear*, 2005, page 339
Image 68. Charles Kroll, *Fred Bear*, 1988, page 78
Image 69. Author
Image 70. Howard Hill, *Hunting The Hard Way*, 1953, page 32
Image 71. Edmund H. Burke, *Archery Handbook*, 1954, page 23
Image 72. Author
Image 73. Ibid.
Image 74. Louis Hochman, *The Complete Archery Book*, 1957, page 24
Image 75. Howard Hill, *Archery Adventures*, 1955, page 35
Imagc 76. Tcd Fry, Oregon
Image 77. Author
Image 78. Howard Hill, *Archery Adventures*, 1955, page 56
Image 79. Craig Ekin, *Howard Hill:The Man and The Legend*, 1982, page 9
Image 80. Bob Wesley, *Traditional Archery Adventures*
Image 81. Cody Roiter, Michigan
Image 82. Howard Hill, *Hunting The Hard Way*, 1953, page 14
Image 83. Craig Ekin
Image 84. Author
Image 85. Bill Negley, *Archer In Africa*, 1989, page 27
Image 86. Ibid., page 60
Image 87. Ibid., page 79
Image 88. Ibid., page 8
Image 89. Ibid., page 135
Image 90. Peter Hathaway Capstick, *A Return to the Long Grass*, 1987
Image 91. Craig Ekin, *Howard Hill: The Man and the Legend*, 1982, page 140
Image 92. Bill Negley, *Archer In Africa*, 1989, page 76
Image 93. Ibid., page 171
Image 94. T. J. Conrads, TBM
Image 95. Bob Swinehart, *In Africa*, 1967, page 46
Image 96. Bob Swinehart, *Sagittarius*, 1970, page 93
Image 97. "My personal reason for any kind of actual hunting is challenge, no matter what the animal or weapon." *Sagittarius*, page 30, Bob Swinehart, *Sagittarius*, 1970, page 146
Image 98. Bob Swinehart, *Sagittarius*, 1970, page 43
Image 99. Bob Swinehart, *In Africa*, 1967, page 11
Image 100. Author
Image 101. Ibid.
Image 102. *44 Years Behind The Bow*, Author
Image 103. Bob Swinehart, *In Africa*, 1967, page 84
Image 104. Ibid., page 34
Image 105. John Schulz, *Straight Shooting*, 2002, page 68
Image 106. Wade Phillips, *Broadheads 1871-1971*, H 34
Image 107. John Schulz, *Hitting 'em Like Howard Hill*, 1979, page 29
Image 108. Author
Image 109. Nate Steen, Idaho
Image 110. Author
Image 111. Ibid.
Image 112. Bob Wesley, *Traditional Archery Adventures*, page 32
Image 113. Angelo Christiano, Montana, Author
Image 114. John Schulz, *Hitting 'em Like Howard Hill*, 1979, page 16
Image 115. Author
Image 116. Ibid.
Image 117. Ibid.
Image 118. Ibid.
Image 119. Ibid.
Image 120. Ibid.
Image 121. Alois Zopf
Image 122. Ibid.
Image 123. Ibid.
Image 124. Ibid.
Image 125. Ibid.
Image 126. Ibid.
Image 127. Ibid.
Image 128. Ibid.
Image 129. Ibid.
Image 130. Ibid.
Image 131. Ibid.
Image 132. Ibid.
Image 133. Ibid.
Image 134. Author
Image 135. Ibid.
Image 136. Michael Sarnitz
Image 137. Ibid.
Image 138. Ibid.
Image 139. Ibid.
Image 140. Ibid.
Image 141. Ibid.
Image 142. Ibid.
Image 143. Ibid.

Image 144. Ibid.
Image 145. Ibid.
Image 146. Author
Image 147. Ibid.
Image 148. Ibid.
Image 149. Ibid.
Image 150. Ibid.
Image 151. Ibid.
Image 152. Ibid.
Image 153. Ibid.
Image 154. Ibid.
Image 155. Ibid.
Image 156. Ibid.
Image 157. Ibid.
Image 158. Ibid.
Image 159. Ibid.
Image 160. Ibid.
Image 161. Ibid.
Image 162. Ibid.
Image 163. Ibid.
Image 164. Ibid.
Image 165. Ibid.
Image 166. Ibid.
Image 167. 1938, Warner Bros. *Howard Hill: The Man and the Legend*, 1982, page 41
Image 168. Lancelyn Green, *The Adventures of Robin Hood*, 2001, Photo by John Holder, page 203
Image 169. Author